4-08-07
Easter Sunday

Dearest Ryan,
I can't believe son
I am giving my to
a book to read first to
tis son to be first the
dear son! where did the
time go? I hope you
enjoy reading to Brian
as much as you. I loved
reading to you.

Love mom

P.S. I know you will
be a wonderful Dad!

This book belongs to:

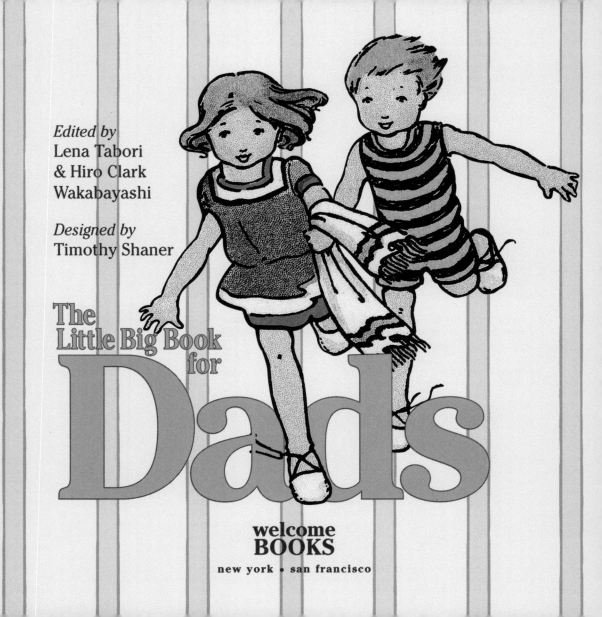

Edited by
**Lena Tabori
& Hiro Clark
Wakabayashi**

Designed by
Timothy Shaner

The
Little Big Book
for
Dads

welcome
BOOKS

new york • san francisco

Published in 2001 by Welcome Books®
An imprint of Welcome Enterprises, Inc.
6 West 18th Street, New York, NY 10011
Tel (212) 989-3200; Fax (212) 989-3205
www.welcomebooks.com

Project Director: Alice Wong
Editorial Assistants: Jacinta O'Halloran, Betsy Davis, Nicholas Liu
Art Assistant: Joanne Berei

Fairy tales retold by Wendy Wax
Music arrangement by Frank Zuback

Library of Congress Control Number: 00-136011
ISBN-10: 0-941807-43-6 / ISBN-13: 978-0-941807-43-2

Printed in China
FIRST EDITION / 10 9 8

Contents

Songs

Fairy Tales

Poetry

Essays

ID's, Tongue Twisters & Jokes

Recipes

Foreword

I had many dads: Folke, to whom I was born in Sweden and who played chess with me in the sauna overlooking a lake outside of Stockholm when I was three; Don, who barbecued in Malibu and pretended to be a horse while I rode on his back in California when I was four; George in New York, who taught me to memorize a poem every week (the first one, when I was eight, "When I am old and gray and full of sleep"), who recorded in his notebooks all of my knock knock jokes and kept track of my grotesque rhymes ("greasy grimy gopher guts…"), and who introduced me to chocolate pudding and whipped cream and Andre Malraux…George, whose second name, Tabori, became mine to simplify things at school and whose name I have treasured ever since.

My daughters had one dad who was at his best when they were small. He put them in the car and drove to Coney Island, letting the movement and the motor rock them to peace when they were babies and couldn't sleep. Later he hoisted them up on his shoulders and strode into Zabars searching for the perfect pastrami and letting them place all the orders. This is the book he would have loved to have, a book filled with jokes for him to tell, activities for him to do with his little ones, stories for him to read, and recipes for him to make.

And it was a book I made with another dad of two daughters: Clark, my business partner of twelve years. He and I have an office of eight people, three of whom are dads. There are five little ones under five and another one on the way. A year ago his wife and I made *The Little Big Book for Moms*. Now it's Dad's turn.

—Lena Tabori

Foreword

In becoming a dad for the first time five years ago, I experienced what a long line of parents before me have surely already encountered: the vast and awesome possibility of a new life as yet unlived. In a child's first gurgling cries there are an immediate hunger and yearning for the world that call for a ceaseless response, an endless resourcefulness, and unlimited patience. All in all, way more than any new parent could anticipate.

The care and nurturing of Chi Chi (Eve), and now also Sylvia, have created a whole new life for all of us, including Alice, our family's devoted and sleep-deprived leader. In this dynamic daily interaction of experience and inexperience, I have had to ponder and search for the things I want my children to have, to know, to feel, to think, to do, to believe—in short, to be. It's an amazing experience, part rediscovery of my own childhood, part exploration of everything else there is in the world for a child to feed on.

To that end, this little big hodge podge of a book is meant as a treasure trove for all dads to dig through. Within its covers many gems are contained, each of great value and each with a gift to excite, inspire, amuse, and engage a child's curiosity. It's a cozy book, one you can curl up on a couch with and share with a pair of page-turning crazy little hands. It's a deliciously plump book, full of tasty morsels to entice all sweet-loving tots.

This collection is an invitation for dads to do what comes naturally to any parent: to see themselves reflected in their children and to take a journey back into that remote but suddenly reborn world, childhood. For me, it's been a series of pleasant surprises: remembering a story or song I once loved; making little edible treats my mother used to make; simply creating with scissors and glue again.

Instinctively, I am always looking within for the best my parents gave me, the most important and lasting of which has been the love of laughter. I remember my

Foreword

parents' laughter. I remember my own and my brother's. And now, nothing is more satisfying to me than Chi Chi's spasms of hilarity or Sylvia's explosive cackles. Mostly, this inspires me to seek ways to bring their laughter out in the world, so that if nothing else, they will later recall their youth with a bright smile and enjoy sudden inner bursts of amusement that ignite again at the briefest spark of a happy memory.

While I dedicate this book to you, my daughters, I also enclose within it a memory along with a wish for you to rediscover it at a later time in your lives. Early in Chi Chi's life I began to make up a song that was inspired by that most routine and repeated of tasks: diaper changing. Slowly over time, the song evolved and grew—line by line, diaper change by diaper change. I sang it for you both and eventually you learned and sang it too, with gusto. It goes like this:

Oh, I've a soggy butt but I'm okay.
I go to sleep and pee the night away.
I wake up early, I bother mum and dad,
I've a soggy butt but I'm glad
To be awake and having lots of fun.
Who the hey cares if I've got a soggy bum.
I like to air it out but never get the chance,
I spend all day in my soggy pants.
Every now and then, they check my little bum,
It's the only time it ever sees the sun.
Oh, I've a soggy butt but I'm okay-y-y-y-y,
Just strap me up and off I go to play!

(Inspired by "The Lumberjack Song" from *Monty Python's Flying Circus*)

This will always make me laugh. I hope it is the same for you.

—Hiro Clark Wakabayashi

13

If the new American father feels
bewildered and even defeated, let
him take comfort from the fact that

whatever he does in any fathering situation he has a fifty percent chance of being right.

—Bill Cosby

Fatherhood

Bill Cosby

Because It's There

It's love, of course, that makes us fathers do it—love for the woman we've married and love for every baby we've ever seen, except the one that threw up on our shoes. And so, in spite of all our reservations about this scary business of reproduction, we must admit that people look happy when they're carrying babies. The male looks especially happy because he has someone to carry it for him, his darling packager.

But his wife is happy too, because she feels she's fulfilling herself as a woman. I've heard so many females say that they became mothers because they wanted to feel like women, as if they felt like longshoremen at all other times. And so many others have said,

"I had the baby because I wanted to see if I could," which sounds like a reason for climbing Mount Everest or breaking the four-minute mile. If a chimpanzee can have a baby, the human female should realize that the feat is something less than an entry for the *Guinness Book of World Records*.

The new father, of course, feels that his mere impregnation of his mate, done every day by otters and apes, is Olympic gold medal stuff. Even if he's afraid of garter snakes, he feels positively heroic. He feels that he and his wife have nobly created something that will last. He never thinks that they may have created one of the top ten underachievers in their town.

■

Almost as Smart as Neanderthals

Before we had children, my wife and I felt educated. She was a college graduate, a child psychology major with a B-plus average, which means, if you ask her a question about a child's behavior, she will give you eighty-five percent of the answer. And I was a physical education major with a child psychology minor at Temple, which means if you ask me a question about a child's behavior, I will advise you to tell the child to take a lap.

Because we were college graduates, we studied things that people have always done naturally, like have children; and so, we decided to have our first child by natural childbirth. Childbirth, of course, *is* a natural thing: the pains come automatically, the muscles contract and push down, and all you need, as they say, is hot water. Neanderthals delivered children without training manuals.

At any rate, these classes give the father a diploma so that he can attend the birth. And what the classes teach him is how to be a cheerleader in the delivery room: how to say, "Push! Push! Push 'em out, shove 'em out, waaay out!"

My wife's job was to keep breathing, but she had studied how to do this in the course, so she was breathing at the top of her class. By the time we had finished the class, we were well prepared for natural childbirth, which means that no drugs can be given to the female during delivery. The father, however, can have all he wants.

One day near the end of the ninth month, my wife came running to me, breathing rapidly, and she cried, "Bill!"

"Push!" I said.

But then I remembered something from the class: You have to go to a hospital. And so we did, at 120 miles an hour, with my wife moaning all the way. When we got to the hospital, we went

Fatherhood

right to the delivery room, where I put the booties on my shoes. Her legs went up into the stirrups, while the obstetrician sat awaiting the delivery, like Johnny Bench.

When the first big pain hit her, I merrily said, "Push!"

Like every man, of course, I had no understanding of how a labor pain really feels. Carol Burnett said, "If you want to know the feeling, just take your bottom lip and pull it over your head."

When the second big pain hit, she cried out and stood up in the stirrups.

"Morphine!" she said. "I want morphine!"

"But dear," I sweetly replied, "you *know* that morphine—"

"*You* shut up! You did this to me!"

And at the next contraction, she told everyone in the delivery room that my parents were never married. Then she continued breathing while I continued cheering from the sidelines: "Push! Push! Push!"

"I don't *want* to push anymore," she said. "Bill, tell them to give me something."

"No, dear, the class forbids—"

"I'm dropping out of *school*!"

"But you can *do* it!"

Meanwhile, Johnny Bench was still sitting there, waiting for the delivery.

"Look!" I suddenly said. "Isn't that the head?"

"I believe it is," he replied.

"Well, go *get* it."

"It's stuck."

"Then get the salad spoons, man."

So he got the salad spoons, the baby came out, and my wife and I were suddenly sharing the greatest moment in our lives. This was what we had asked God for; this was what we wanted to see if we could make. And I looked at it lovingly as they started to clean it off, but it wasn't getting any better.

And then I went over to my wife, kissed her gently on the lips, and said, "Darling, I love you very much. You just had a lizard."

■

Like the Marines, Be Prepared

I guess the real reason that my wife and I had children is the same reason that Napoleon had for invading Russia: it seemed like a good idea at the time. Since then, however, I've had some doubts, primarily about my intelligence. I began entertaining these doubts when my first daughter was about eighteen months old. Every time I went into her room, she would take some round plastic thing from her crib and throw it on the floor. Then I would pick it up, wipe it off, and hand it back to her so she could throw it back to the floor.

"Don't throw that on the floor, honey," I'd tell her. "Do you understand Daddy? Don't throw that on the floor."

Then I would give it back to her and she would throw it again. Picking it up once more, wiping it off, and returning it to her, I again would say, "Look, I just *told* you not to throw this on the floor, didn't I?"

And, of course, she would listen carefully to me and then throw it again.

This little game is wonderful exercise for the father's back, but it is his *mind* that needs developing. Sometimes a father needs ten or fifteen droppings before he begins to understand that he should *leave* the thing on the floor—or maybe put the child down there too.

During this little game, the child has been thinking: *This person is a lot of fun. He's not too bright, but a lot of fun.*

■

What Are Little Boys Made Of?

What are little boys made of, made of?

What are little boys made of?

"Snaps and snails, and
puppy-dogs' tails;

And that's what little
boys are made of."

20

What are little girls
   made of, made of?

What are little girls
   made of?

"Sugar and spice, and all that's nice;

And that's what little girls are
   made of."

What Are Little Girls Made Of?

Rockabye

by Shel Silverstein

Rockabye baby, in the treetop.
Don't you know a treetop
Is no safe place to rock?
And who put you up there,
And your cradle too?
Baby, I think someone down here's
Got it in for you.

One Two
by Shel Silverstein

One two, buckle my shoe.
    "Buckle your *own* shoe!"
Who said that?
    "I did. What are you doing with those silly buckles
    on your shoes anyway?"
Three, four, shut the door.
    "*You* shut it—you *opened* it."
Er . . . five, six, pick up sticks.
    "Why should I pick them up—do you think I'm your
    slave? Buckle my shoe, shut the door, pick up sticks,
    next thing you'll be telling me to lay them straight."
But it's only a poem . . . Nine, ten, a big fat . . .
    oh never mind.

Pop! Goes the Weasel!

All a - round the cob - bler's bench, the

mon - key chased the wea - sel. The

mon - key thought 'twas all ____ in fun,

Pop! goes the wea - sel.

25

The Gingerbread Boy

Once upon a time there were a little old woman and a little old man who lived in a little old house. The little old man could often be found dozing in his chair (making little old snores) while the little old lady brewed tea in a little old kettle and made meals in a little old pan.

One morning, the little old woman and the little old man received a telegram saying their grandson was coming to visit.

"I know!" said the little old woman. "I'll bake a gingerbread boy for him."

The little old woman mixed the gingerbread batter, shaped it into a boy, and slid it into the oven, leaving the door slightly open by mistake.

"I must go to the market," the little old woman said to the little old man. "Take the gingerbread boy out in ten minutes."

"Yes, dear," said the little old man. But five minutes later, he was fast asleep.

"Hey!" shouted gingerbread boy, who was getting really hot. He peered out of the oven but the little old woman who had made

The Gingerbread Boy

him was nowhere in sight, and the little old man was snoring loudly. The gingerbread boy climbed out onto the stove between the little old kettle and the little old pan and looked around. "It's boring here," he said. He raced out the door, and ran and ran until he reached a group of children playing in a field. The children saw him and licked their lips.

"*Yum!*" said a girl. But before she could break off an arm, the gingerbread boy ran away, calling:

"I am a little gingerbread boy. I have run away from a little old woman and a little old man, a little old kettle and a little old pan, and I can run away from you, I can, I can." And so he ran and ran and came to an old brown cow drooling with hunger.

"*Moo!*" went the cow. But before he could nip off an ear, the gingerbread boy ran away, calling:

"I am a little gingerbread boy. I have run away from a little old woman and a little old man, a little old kettle and a little old pan, a field full of children, and I can run away from you, I can, I can." And so he ran and ran and came to a sly fox.

"I am a little Gingerbread Boy," he said to the fox. "I have run away from a little old woman and a little old man, a little old

The Gingerbread Boy

kettle and a little old pan, a field full of children and an old brown cow, and I can run away from you, I can, I can." But as he ran, so did the fox—and foxes are fast! Soon they came to a wide river.

"Would you like to go across?" the fox asked, jumping into the water.

"Sure," said the gingerbread boy, catching his breath.

"Climb on my tail," the fox suggested.

The gingerbread boy did just that. But as the water got deeper, the tail got wetter.

"You'll stay dryer if you climb on my back," the fox suggested.

The gingerbread boy climbed on the fox's back. Soon the water deepened.

"You'd better climb on my nose," the fox suggested.

So the gingerbread boy climbed on the fox's nose—which was a *big* mistake. For the fox opened his mouth, and gobbled the gingerbread boy up!

"Delicious," said the fox, satisfied. "Gingerbread boys are meant to be eaten, not to be out running around." And he curled up under a tree, drifted off into a nap, and dreamt about more scrumptious gingerbread boys.

Five Toes

This little pig went to market;

This little pig stayed at home;

This little pig had roast beef;

This little pig had none;

This little pig said, "Wee, wee!

I can't find my way home."

Is That a Box?

Never throw away a cardboard box! The imaginary play a child can have with a box is endless. Use brown paper to cover up boxes that have markings. Then, with a few cuts and some new marks, your child can be master of his or her own house, a racecar driver, or a chef. The instructions below are just a start—think boat, sled, castle, television set, refrigerator, puppet theater. . . .

cardboard boxes, masking tape, scissors, markers, glue

PLAYHOUSE

1. Tape and secure together the flaps of a large appliance box.
2. Draw door and windows on the sides of the box and cut along their outlines, leaving hinges of cardboard so that they can open and close.
3. Have your child help decorate by drawing bricks, curtains, or window boxes on the outside.

RACECAR

1. You will need a box large enough for a child to sit in. Cut away the flaps and cut down the top of the box to the chest level of your sitting child.
2. From the extra cardboard, cut out a steering wheel for your child to hold.

You can also cut out a play key.
3. Cut out four wheels from the extra cardboard for your child to glue on.
4. Make an L-shaped cut in one side of the box to make a door, folding back the flap to create a hinge-like effect.
5. Draw a dashboard on the inside of the box, complete with speedometer and gauges. Red buttons for "eject" and "maximum speed" are fun additions.
6. Don't forget the outside of the car! Add headlights and fenders; decorate with sponsor logos, numbers, and favorite shapes.

KITCHEN STOVE

1. Set a large box whichever way the height best suits your child, but make sure there is a flat surface on top.
2. Draw on circles for burners and knobs.
3. Cut an oven door into the front.

A Pancake of Your Own

Use a spoon (or chicken baster) to dribble your child's initial—backwards—onto the pan a few seconds before you spoon on the circle of pancake batter. When you flip the pancake, the initial will appear on the other side. You can also make animal outlines, dollar signs, or heart shapes using this method. A good pancake pan is a great help. This recipe is from three great dads: Philip, Rob, and Franco.

*1 1/2 cups unbleached white flour
(or corn meal)
1 tablespoon sugar
1/4 tablespoon salt
1 tablespoon baking powder
3 eggs, separated
1/4 cup melted butter (easily done
    in the microwave)
2 cups milk*

1. Preheat oven to 200°F and put a plate in to warm.
2. In a large bowl, combine dry ingredients.
3. In another bowl, beat egg yolks with the melted butter and milk. Stir into the flour mixture.
4. Beat egg whites until they are fluffy and fold them into the batter.
5. Heat a lightly buttered frying pan over medium-high heat.
6. Dribble your initial or shape onto the pan first. Then drop a large spoonful of batter on top of the browning initial. When the bubbles start to dry, flip and brown on the other side.
7. Keep pancakes warm in the oven until ready to serve.
8. Serve with your favorite toppings—applesauce, maple syrup, lemon juice and powdered sugar, or your favorite jam. (If you are a Swede, it has to be lingonberries; if you are Hungarian, apricot jam will be your choice).

Serves 4 to 6

Eggs are the Best

Trust me, you can't go wrong with eggs and there are endless variations. Great scrambled eggs are a must and egg-soaked bread—french toast—is divine. And then there are One-Eyed Sailors. Philip Patrick, father of the charming Eleanor, told me about his dad making them while his mom slept in. Then Franco (my guy) said, "No, no, no. That's an Egg in a Nest and Jay (his son) had it for breakfast with maple syrup when he was a little guy." So, whatever you call it, it's a big hit.

Great Scrambled Eggs

4 eggs
1/4 cup milk
1/2 cup diced tomatoes
1/4 cup grated cheddar or Swiss cheese
salt and pepper to taste
1 tablespoon butter

1. Break eggs into a bowl and add milk. Beat with a fork until the eggs are frothy, then add tomatoes, cheese, and salt and pepper.
2. Melt the butter in a nonstick frying pan. When it sizzles, lower the heat, pour in the egg mixture, and move it around with the back of the fork. Cook until the egg forms soft curds and serve immediately.

Serves 2

Other tasty additions to scrambled eggs: small pieces of ham or bacon; sauteed and chopped zucchini, peppers, mushrooms, or onions; mozzarella, havarti, or cottage cheese; chopped parsley, oregano, basil, thyme, or chives.

Eggs are the Best

French Toast

6 eggs
1/2 cup milk
dash cinnamon or nutmeg, or 1/2
  teaspoon vanilla extract (optional)
12 thick slices challah or your
  favorite softer-type bread
4 tablespoons butter

1. Put warming plate in a 250°F oven.
2. In a wide bowl, whisk together eggs, milk, and optional seasoning.
3. Soak both sides of the bread until completely soaked.
4. Heat a large frying pan over high heat for 20 seconds and then reduce heat to medium. Add the butter.
5. When the butter stops sizzling, add pieces of soaked bread. Cook until golden brown, about 3 to 4 minutes on each side.
6. Keep warm in the oven and serve immediately when the rest of the toast is done. Serve with applesauce, syrup, or powdered sugar and cinnamon.

Serves 6

One-Eyed Sailors

4 slices challah, rye, or another
  favorite bread
4 tablespoons butter
4 eggs

1. Use the rim of a glass to press and cut a circle out of the middle of each slice of bread. (You can save the circles to make French Toast).
2. In a non-stick frying pan, heat the butter over low heat until it is melted and the pan is hot.
3. Put slices of bread in the pan.
4. Crack eggs, one at a time, into a small bowl and slide each egg into the hole in each slice of bread.
5. Cook for a few minutes until the white of the egg is firm. Then flip and cook for a couple of minutes on the other side until the yolk is as firm as you like.
6. Serve with maple syrup.

Serves 2

Food

What do you get
when you put three
ducks in a box?
A box of quackers.

What kind of crackers
do firemen like in
their soup?
Firecrackers.

What starts with "t,"
ends with "t," and is
filled with "t"?
A teapot.

What do you call a
train loaded with
bubble gum?
A chew-chew train.

Why did the boy throw
butter out the window?
*He wanted to
see a butterfly.*

Why is a cook mean?
*Because he beats eggs,
mashes potatoes, and
whips cream.*

What did the baby corn
say to the mama corn?
I want my pop-corn!

What do you
call tired popcorn?
Pooped-corn.

What do you call a
peanut in outer space?
An astronut.

What happens when
you tell an egg a joke?
It cracks up!

How do you make a
milkshake?
Say BOO! to a cow.

Why did the cow
eat a chocolate bar?
*Because he wanted to
make chocolate milk.*

Why did the cookie
go to the doctor?
Because he felt crummy.

What do you call a dog
on fire?
A hot dog.

Jokes

Betty Botter bo

Betty Botter bought some butter,
    But, she said, the butter's bitter;
If I put it in my batter
    It will make my batter bitter,
But a bit of better butter,
    That would make my batter better.
So she bought a bit of butter
    Better than her bitter butter,
And she put it in her batter
    And the batter was not bitter.
So t'was better Betty Botter
    Bought a bit of better butter.

There Was an

There was an
old woman who
lived in a shoe.

She had so many
children she didn't
know what to do.

Old Woman

She gave them
some broth
without
any bread.

She kissed them all
soundly and
put them to bed.

The Pied Piper of Hamelin

nce upon a time the village of Hamelin sat upon the banks of a great river. The people who lived there considered themselves lucky, for they were all rich, ate the finest foods, wore the most stylish clothes, and lived in the most elegant houses. But even so, Hamelin had a big problem: rats—mean, gray rats with sharp, gray teeth everywhere you looked. These rats were very smart, and they never walked into the traps or ate the poison the villagers set out for them. Instead, they nibbled on food, clothing, and even toes! Determined to find a solution, the people of Hamelin went straight to the mayor.

"LET'S GET CATS TO KILL THE RATS!" the mayor proposed.

Everyone cheered, proud that they had elected such a firm and smart man.

Within a week, everyone in town had at least three cats. (They never bought just one of anything.)

For two weeks, the mayor's plan worked splendidly. The cats ate the rats, and the people of Hamelin forgot their worries. But then something strange happened. The cats started dying and the

The Pied Piper of Hamelin

rats started multiplying. Soon, there were more rats than ever—everywhere you looked! A meeting was called in the Town Hall.

"We've tried poison and traps," said a woman.

"And thousands of cats," said a man.

"How can we get rid of the rats?" the people cried out.

The mayor shrugged helplessly.

Suddenly, there was a knock at the door. When the mayor's assistant opened it, a tall, thin stranger dressed in brightly colored silks entered the room. A long feather stuck out of his purple hat, and he carried a beautiful, golden pipe.

"I am the Pied Piper," the stranger said, "and I've freed other villages of beetles and bats. Pay me a thousand gold coins, and I'll get rid of all your rats!"

"We'll give you *fifty* thousand gold coins if you succeed!" said the mayor.

"Very well," said the Pied Piper. "By daybreak tomorrow, there won't be a rat left in Hamelin!" Then he was gone.

That evening at sunset, the magical tones of a pipe wafted through the village of Hamelin. Rats scampered out of every nook and cranny in every house, shop, and office, to flock at the heels of the Pied Piper. When he reached the river, the Pied Piper

The Pied Piper of Hamelin

continued to play as he waded straight in. By the time the water reached his chest, all the rats had drowned and every last one of them was swept away by the current.

"I'd like my fifty thousand gold coins," the Pied Piper told the mayor the next morning.

"Fifty thousand!" exclaimed the greedy mayor, for, though the village had money, it was needed to maintain the fancy gardens, parks, and museums. Now that the rats were gone, why pay the piper what he had promised, he reasoned; the town's problem had already been solved.

"Then give me a thousand gold coins, as I originally requested!" said the Piper, annoyed.

"I'll give you fifty," said the mayor, "which I think is very generous indeed."

The townspeople agreed, for they loved their gardens, parks, and museums. "You should simply be grateful for what you get," they said.

"You can keep your fifty measly gold coins!" cried the Piper. "You broke your promise, and you'll soon regret it." Then he disappeared.

That night, the people of Hamelin slept soundly, for they no longer worried about rats crawling into bed with them. When the sound of the Pied Piper's pipe wafted through the streets, only

the children heard it. In their pajamas, the children of Hamelin—from toddlers to teenagers—left their houses and followed the Pied Piper to a dark forest at the edge of town, mesmerized by the magical tones of his pipe.

The Pied Piper led the procession through the forest to the foot of a majestic mountain. He played three mysterious notes, and a giant piece of the mountain creaked open like a door. In he marched, playing his golden pipe, with the children at his heels. When they were all inside, the mountain closed up behind them.

"Wait for me!" cried a boy with a twisted ankle, who hadn't been quick enough. But the door was nowhere to be found.

When the sun came up, the boy returned to the village of Hamelin, where everyone was looking for their children—including the mayor, whose eight sons and eight daughters had all disappeared during the night.

The boy with the twisted ankle told everyone what had happened. The mayor and the townspeople wailed and cried for their children, but it was no use.

The Pied Piper and the children of Hamelin were never seen again, and, to this day, no one has ever found an entrance to the mountain.

Where Did You Come From, Baby Dear?

by George MacDonald

Where did you come from, baby dear?
Out of the everywhere into here.

Where did you get your eyes so blue?
Out of the sky as I came through.

What makes the light in them sparkle and spin?
Some of the starry spikes left in.

Where did you get that little tear?
I found it waiting when I got here.

What makes your forehead so smooth and high?
A soft hand stroked it as I went by.

What makes your cheek like a warm white rose?
I saw something better than anyone knows.

Whence that three-cornered smile of bliss?
Three angels gave me at once a kiss.

Where did you get this pearly ear?
God spoke, and it came out to hear.

Where did you get those arms and hands?
Love made itself into hooks and bands.

Feet, whence did you come, you darling things?
From the same box as the cherubs' wings.

How did they all just come to be you?
God thought about me, and so I grew.

But how did you come to us, you dear?
God thought about you, and so I am here.

Being a Father

Winston Groom

This is a story of selfishness and redemption, of anxiety and love, of resignation and wonderment. It's the story of Carolina Montgomery Groom, age fourteen months, and her papa.

"It will change your life forever!"

This was the cry I'd heard through the years whenever having children was mentioned. It was disturbing, if not frightening. I didn't want my life "changed forever." It was scary enough getting married again. When you get married you have to give up things and at heart I am a selfish person. But life's a trade-off and if I hadn't married the woman I love she would have married somebody else and I would have made the stupidest mistake of my existence . . .

At 2:05 P.M. Carolina Montgomery Groom arrived in the world. Everybody was laughing and crying. I bit a hole in my lip. Cheering began in the waiting room. I don't remember much except that at some point the nurse handed her to me. I couldn't believe she was so tiny (though that was soon to change—big time). I gave her to Anne-Clinton, whose eyes were glistening and I never recalled a sweeter smile on her face as she cradled her in her arms.

The nurse finally gave her back to me and said we needed to get her to the nursery while the doctor finished up his business. I took her in my arms and with me in the lead we made our way back down corridors until I saw all our friends lined up outside the glass wall of the nursery. There was a door to the hall and I ignorantly started to take Carolina through it to show her to

Being a Father

the friends up close, but the horrified nurse restrained me. It had been a long day, but all was truly right with the world. Everybody's heard about the "miracle of birth," but when I finally got to bed that night I lay in awe of what had just happened in our lives. There was suddenly a new, living, breathing little human on the planet among what is now supposed to be six billion other living breathing humans. But this one was ours, by our own creation, and I vowed then and there that she was going to get all the love and care and devotion in my power to give her her chance in the world.

"It's going to change your life forever!" Again the mighty cry swelled up worse than the chorus from the Trojan Women.

At first I was a bit mystified. She was so tiny, Carolina. I didn't know what to do and in fact there wasn't much I could do. We had a nurse and between her and Anne-Clinton and Wren they had things well in hand, so I sort of hung around with the dogs who didn't seem to know what to make of it either. Then one morning Anne-Clinton brought her into bed and we were there, all three of us, and she smiled for the first time I could recall. That was it for me!

Oh, they grow so fast! Everybody says that, but it's too true.

Carolina quickly went off the doctor's charts in height. (Both Anne-Clinton and I are tall.) For her first birthday I bought her a rocking horse. Not just any rocking horse but I splurged on an antique English rocking horse that's actually the size of a small pony. When they delivered it, Anne-Clinton was beside herself.

Being a Father

"She won't be able to ride that thing until she's three!" she laughed.

I have begun doing all the things I swore always not to do. I carry around baby pictures and show them to people, a thing I detested in others before this. I talk baby talk to Carolina and delight in everything she does. From what people say, she's the best-behaved baby they can remember. She doesn't cry much except when she's hungry, and when she laughs and smiles—which is most of the time—she lights up the universe. She has big blue eyes and strawberry blonde hair and can crawl faster than I can walk. I revel in every new task she learns; she adores picture books and likes to draw and paint and eat crayons. She's so beautiful that someday she's going to accidentally break some boy's heart, but not mine.

I look forward to teaching her to ride and sail and fish and play tennis and to go for long walks in the mountain forests. And if I have to go to Little League or soccer or whatever, I'll do it joyfully. I only hope to live long enough to see how she turns out, but if not that's okay too. I've had enough joy since that day she came into our lives to last a lifetime. When she crawls in bed with us in the morning and says "Papa," my heart leaps; and then she'll do something nice like stick her finger in your eye. Do you think I would trade it?

"It's going to change your life forever!" They are right, of course, and so what? You think I'm not looking forward to it?

■

Knee Rides

Knee rides are one of the first games children adore. You can bounce older babies gently on knees to elicit great belly laughs. Give older children a real "wild" ride on your foot, holding onto their hands.

This is the way the ladies ride,
Tripity trot, tripity trot
On their way to town.
(bounce child gently on knee)

This is the way the gentlemen ride,
Gallop-a-gallop, gallop-a-gallop
On their way to town.
(bounce faster)

This is the way the farmers ride!
Clompity-clomp, clomp, clomp!
On their way to town.
(bounce really fast)

Trot, trot to Boston town
   to get a stick of candy.
One for you, and one for me,
   and one for Dicky Dandy.

Ride a cock-horse to Branbury Cross,
   To buy little Johnny a galloping horse;
It trots behind and it ambles before,
   And Johnny shall ride till he can ride no more.

The Hokey Pokey

You put your right hand in, you put your right hand out, you put your right hand in and you shake it all a-bout. You do the Ho - key Po - key and you turn your-self a - round; That's what it's all a - bout!

2. You put your left hand in . . .

3. Right foot in

4. Left foot in

5. Right shoulder in

6. Left shoulder in

7. Right hip in

8. Left hip in

9. Head in

10. Whole self in

The Ant and the Cricket

 nce upon a hot summer, on the tip of a leafy branch, lounged a cricket. All day and all night, she sang cheerful songs while watching a long line of ants slave away on the ground below.

"Hey, down there!" she called between songs. "How can you work in this heat?"

"We're . . . storing . . . food . . . for . . . the . . . winter," answered an ant, struggling under the weight of a piece of grain.

"But winter is months away!" shouted the cricket. "You've got to learn to relax."

"We can't," explained another ant from beneath a morsel of sugar. "It takes us all summer to fill our winter pantry. And we'll only make it through the winter if our pantry is full."

The cricket shrugged. "As I always say, summer is for singing, winter is for worrying," she said, nibbling a bright green leaf. "Take a break, and I'll teach you a song."

"Thanks, but no thanks," said an ant, rolling a bread crumb in front of him.

The Ant and the Cricket

All summer long, the cricket sang while the ants worked. Soon autumn came and the leaves fell from the trees. The cricket climbed down from the bare tree. She was too hungry and tired to sing more than a line or two of a song.

"Brrr," she said, making her way through crunching leaves. "It's getting chilly." She wished the ants were still around—not that they'd been great company, but at least she could talk to them.

Soon an early frost covered the fields, and the cricket felt hungrier than ever. She fed on the few dry stalks left on the frozen ground, but that barely gave her enough strength to move. Her throat was so dry she couldn't sing a single note.

Then it began to snow. Trembling and famished, the cricket curled up under a tree, closed her eyes, and dreamed of the carefree summer days. She awoke to the faint sound of singing. It was coming from a speck of light in the distance. Gathering all her strength, she made her way toward the light.

When she arrived at the front door of a tiny house at the foot of a pine tree, she managed a faint knock. No one heard her. "Open the door!" she cried, as loudly as she could. "I'm starving. I need food!"

The Ant and the Cricket

The singing stopped, and an ant peered out the window. "Who's out there?" he asked.

"It's me—the cricket," the cricket said. "I'm cold and hungry, and I have no place to go." She sneezed.

"We worked hard all summer while you sang songs," said the ants, gathering around the window.

"Sorry, there's no free food here," said an ant, munching on a corn kernel.

Then they went back to their singing.

"Poor me," the cricket moaned, wishing she had collected food while it was plentiful. She collapsed on the doorstep.

The next day, a small ant peered out the window. "That lazy cricket's still here!" he cried. "And she looks too weak to move."

At last, the ants took pity on the cricket and, gathering all their strength, they carried her into their home. They fed her until she gained her strength back, and then invited her to stay for the rest of the winter—under one condition: She'd have to serve them all their food until the first signs of spring.

Insects

Whether they love them or scream at their sight, all children are fascinated by bugs. Take your child on an expedition to learn more about these six-legged creatures, and watch new friendships form. Search for these insects under rocks, in the garden, near a pond, or in the darkness after dusk. Your child can catch fireflies in a jar (poking holes in the lid, of course) and keep them by the bed for a night, shedding light on fears both of insects and the dark.

FIREFLY

GRASSHOPPER

PRAYING MANTIS

BUMBLEBEE

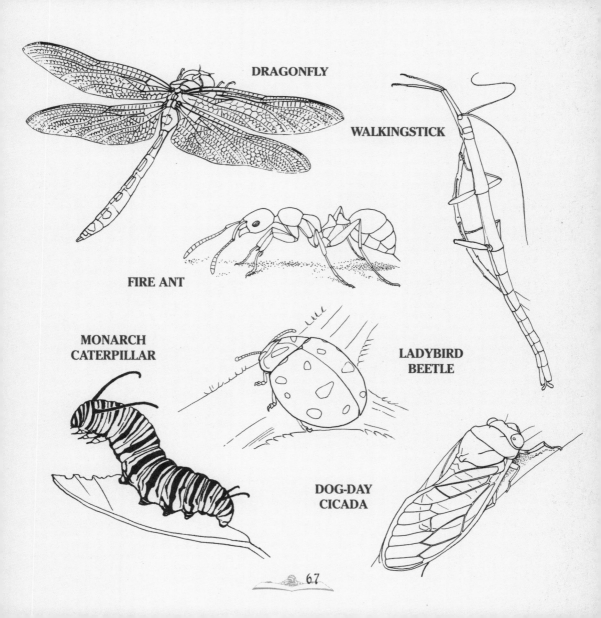

DRAGONFLY

WALKINGSTICK

FIRE ANT

MONARCH
CATERPILLAR

LADYBIRD
BEETLE

DOG-DAY
CICADA

Insect Collecting

Of all the animals on the earth, there are none more plentiful than bugs. You and your child can find thousands of varieties of bugs in your very own backyard or local park. The hunt is only half the fun because some bugs make fine pets, even if only briefly.

EARTHWORMS
jar, loose soil, water, leaves, flashlight, red plastic wrap

1. Fill a jar about three-quarter's full with soil, adding a little water to create a moist consistency. Do not pack the dirt. Put a few leaves on top.
2. Worms are found most easily in the dark after a rainstorm. They tend to stay in damp, cool places, so check underneath rocks and logs. Put the flashlight in red plastic wrap since worms are less sensitive to red light. Carefully scoop up worms with your hands and place them into the jar. Wash your hands afterwards.
3. Put the worms in a dark place, like a closet, for a few days to let them settle down. When you take them out again, they will have started their intricate burrowing. You can add cabbage leaves or other leafy vegetables for food, but be sure to remove rotting food periodically.
4. Keep the jar in a dark place in between viewings and keep the soil moist. Earthworms can have as many as 15 babies about every 5 weeks and can live up to 10 years! It will be necessary to release worms back outside as they multiply.

FIREFLIES
jar, flashlight

1. On a summer evening, look for the telltale green light of the firefly. If it's moving around (meaning that the fly is male), study the pattern of the light and try to imitate it with your flashlight. He will fly up to you, thinking you are a female firefly answering his light signal.
2. Try to catch the fly with cupped hands. This may take some time, but fireflies tend to be rather friendly, at least compared to other bugs.
3. If you manage to catch one, place it carefully in a jar, covering the open end. Only keep it there a little while because fireflies do not survive long in captivity.

70.

Old Mother Goose

Old Mother Goose, when

She wanted to wander,

Would ride through the air

On a very fine gander.

An Alphabet

by Edward Lear

A
A was once an apple pie,
Pidy
Widy
Tidy
Pidy
Nice insidy
   Apple Pie!

B
B was once a little bear,
Beary!
Wary!
Hairy!
Beary!
Taky cary!
Little Bear!

C
C was once a little cake,
Caky
Baky
Maky
Caky
Taky Caky,
Little Cake!

D
D was once a little doll,
Dolly
Molly
Polly
Nolly
Nursy Dolly
Little Doll!

E
E was once a little eel,
Eely
Weely
Peely
Eely
Twirly, Tweely
Little Eel!

F
F was once a little fish,
Fishy
Wishy
Squishy
Fishy
In a Dishy
Little Fish!

G
G was once a little goose,
Goosy
Moosy
Boosey
Goosey
Waddly-woosy
little Goose!

H
H was once a little hen,
Henny
Chenny
Tenny
Henny
Eggsy-any
Little Hen?

I

I was once a bottle of ink,
Inky
Dinky
Thinky
Inky
Blacky Minky
Bottle of Ink!

J

J was once a jar of jam,
Jammy
Mammy
Clammy
Jammy
Sweety—Swammy
Jar of Jam!

K

K was once a little kite,
Kity

Whity
Flighty
Kity
Out of Sighty—
Little Kite!

L

L was once a little lark,
Larky!
Marky!
Harky!
Larky!
In the Parky,
Little Lark!

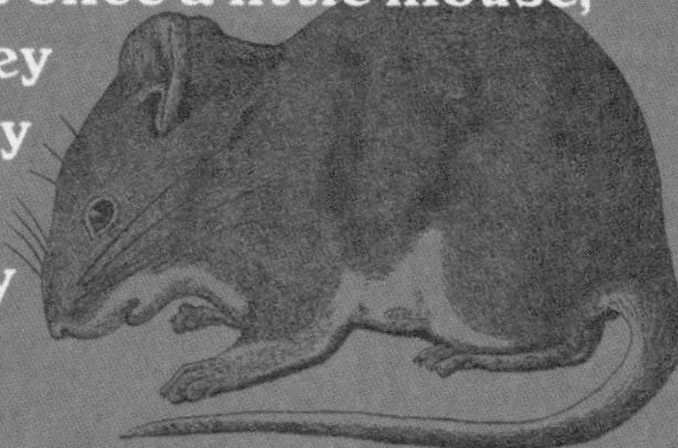

M

M was once a little mouse,
Mousey
Bousey
Sousy
Mousy

In the Housy
Little Mouse!

N 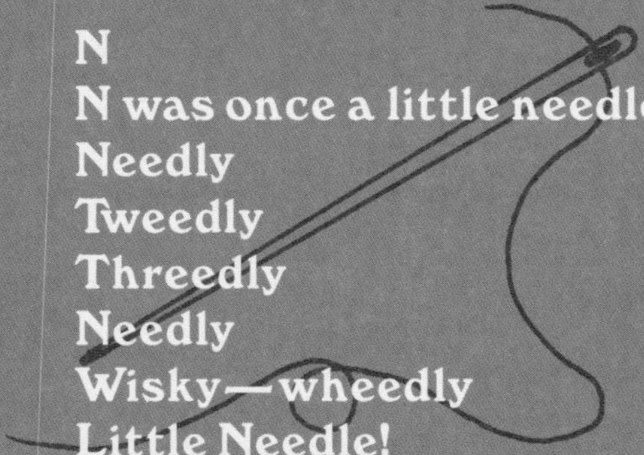
N was once a little needle,
Needly
Tweedly
Threedly
Needly
Wisky—wheedly
Little Needle!

O 
O was once a little owl,
Owly
Prowly
Howly
Owly
Browny fowly
Little Owl!

P 
P was once a little pump,
Pumpy
Slumpy
Flumpy
Pumpy
Dumpy, Thumpy
Little Pump!

Q 
Q was once a little quail,
Quaily
Faily
Daily
Quaily
Stumpy-taily
Little Quail!

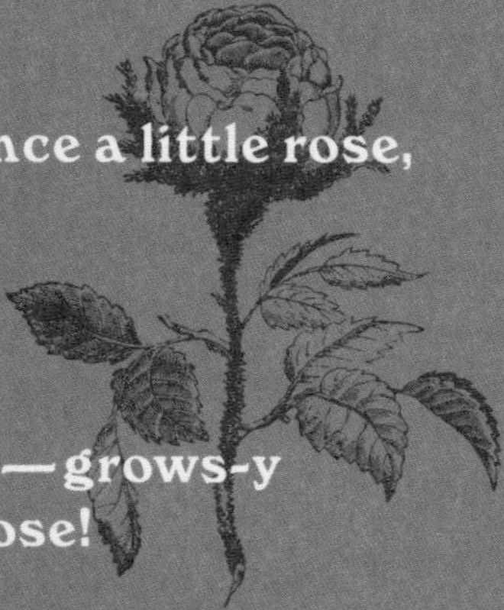

R

R was once a little rose,
Rosy
Posy
Nosy
Rosy
Blows-y—grows-y
Little Rose!

S

S was once a little shrimp,
Shrimpy
Nimpy
Flimpy
Shrimpy
Jumpy—jimpy
Little Shrimp!

T

T was once a little thrush,
Thrushy!
Hushy!
Bushy!
Thrushy!
Flitty—Flushy
Little Thrush!

U

U was once a little urn,
Urny
Burny
Turny
Urny
Bubbly—burny
Little Urn!

V

V was once a little vine,
Viny
Winy
Twiny
Viny

Twisty-twiny
Little Vine!

W
W was once a whale,
Whaly
Scaly
Shaly
Whaly
Tumbly-taily
Mighty Whale!

X
X was once a great
        king Xerxes,
Xerxy
Perxy
Turxy
Xerxy
Linxy Lurxy
Great King Xerxes!

Y
Y was once a little yew,
Yewdy
Fewdy
Crudy
Yewdy
Growdy, grewdy,
Little Yew!

Z
Z was once a piece of zinc,
Tinky
Winky
Blinky
Tinky
Tinkly Minky
Piece of Zinc!

This Old Man

This old man, He played one, He played nick - nack

on my thumb; With a nick - nack, pad - dy whack,

give a dog a bone, This old man came rol - ling home.

2. This old man, he played two,
       He played nick-nack on my shoe;
   With a nick-nack paddy whack,
       give a dog a bone,
   This old man came rolling home.

3. . . . three . . . on my knee

4. . . . four . . . on my door

5. . . . five . . . on my hive

6. . . . six . . . on my sticks

7. . . . seven . . . up in heaven

8. . . . eight . . . on my gate

9. . . . nine . . . on my spine

10. . . . ten . . . once again

Baa, Baa, Black Sheep

Baa, baa, black sheep,
Have you any wool?
Yes sir, yes sir,
Three bags full;

One for my master,
One for my dame,
But none for the little boy
Who cries in the lane.

The Fox and the Crow

nce upon a branch sat a crow with a fresh chunk of cheese in her beak. She was saving it for her dinner. "Hello, Crow," said a sly voice from below.

The crow looked down and was startled to see a fox looking up at her. (She didn't know that the mischievous fox had been watching her for quite some time.)

"Your coat is as shiny as silk," the fox said admiringly.

The crow fluffed her feathers proudly.

"Your wings are as delicate as lace," the fox said softly.

The crow gracefully lifted her wings.

"And your eyes are as bright as diamonds," the fox said lovingly.

The crow winked at the fox. She had never met a fox with such a fine eye for beauty.

"You're so perfectly formed," said the fox, "it's too bad you don't have a voice."

"But I do!" said the crow, not noticing that the cheese had fallen from her beak. "Caw, caw, caw . . . caw!" she sang out.

The Fox and the Crow

"Caw, caw, CAW!"

She waited for the fox to tell her she had the sweetest voice he'd ever heard—but the fox was nowhere in sight. Neither was the cheese.

"I've been tricked!" the crow said angrily, realizing that the fox had run off with her cheese.

"You deserved it," said a caterpillar that had seen the whole thing. "It's no wonder the fox didn't compliment you on your brains."

Bird Feeders

Making your own bird feeder is not only a good way to help the feathered ones living in your neighborhood, it's also a good way to acquaint your child with Mother Nature. Place the bird feeder near a window or in a tree in a frequented spot near your home. Your child can watch and learn to identify the birds that come to appreciate his or her offering.

HUMMINGBIRD FEEDER

orange, knife

1. Slice an orange in half and pierce it onto a sturdy twig on a tree. The cut side of the orange should face out so that hummingbirds (or butterflies) can easily sip from the orange.

PEANUT BUTTER FEEDER

peanut butter, bird seed, pinecone, string

1. Spread peanut butter in the crevices of a large pinecone.
2. Roll the pinecone in some birdseed, making sure that a significant amount of the seed sticks.
3. Tie a piece of very strong string to the pinecone, and hang it from the branch of a tree near your home.

MILK CARTON FEEDER

1-quart milk carton, bird seed, a small stick, string, scissors

1. Clean and dry the milk carton. Cut out and remove two parallel sides of the carton, leaving about three inches at the bottom, and several inches at the top of each side. The space that is cut out should be large enough for a bird to perch in.
2. Poke a hole through the top of the two sides that are still intact, and run the stick through it.
3. Tie a string to each side of the stick (where it sticks out the sides of the milk carton).
4. Fill the bottom with seed and hang the feeder from a tree branch.

Birds

Birds are Nature's musicians, boasting their songs from the tops of trees, telephone poles, lampposts, and piers. Whether you live in the city, the country, or somewhere in between, chances are you encounter at least one of these feathered friends on a daily basis. Introduce your child to the birds that live in your neighborhood, letting him or her hear and enjoy the different songs. In time your child will be able to identify by sound alone the source of the twittering outside the window at the crack of dawn.

WOODPECKER

PIGEON

CARDINAL

HOUSE SPARROW

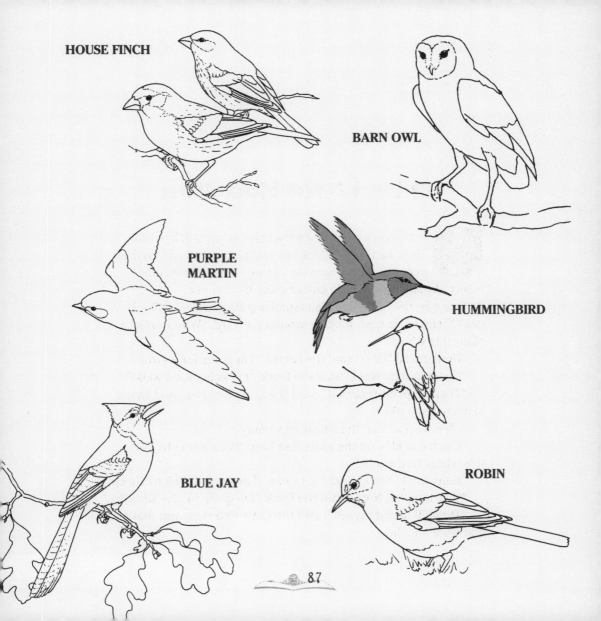

HOUSE FINCH

BARN OWL

PURPLE
MARTIN

HUMMINGBIRD

BLUE JAY

ROBIN

8.7

The Little Red Hen

nce upon a time, in a very noisy farmyard, lived the Little Red Hen. "Cluck cluck! Cluck cluck!" she chirped every day, from sunrise to sunset, as she waddled busily about with her little chicks close behind her.

One day, the Little Red Hen found a grain of wheat. "Cluck cluck!" she exclaimed, looking around the yard. "Who wants to plant this wheat?"

"Honk honk! Not I," said the Goose. "I'm going for a swim."

"Quack quack! Not I," said the Duck. "I'm going for a walk."

"Then I'll plant it myself," said the Little Red Hen. And that's just what she did.

A few weeks later, the wheat was ready.

"Cluck cluck!" said the Little Red Hen. "Who wants to take this wheat to the mill?"

"Honk honk! Not I," said the Goose. "I'm going to talk to Sheep."

"Quack quack! Not I," said the Duck. "I'm going to play with Pig."

"Then I'll take it myself," said the Little Red Hen. And that's just what she did.

The Little Red Hen

A few days later, the wheat had been made into flour.

"Cluck cluck!" said the Little Red Hen. "Who wants to bake bread with this flour?"

"Honk honk! Not I," said the Goose. "I'm going sunbathing."

"Quack quack! Not I," said the Duck. "I'm going to take a nap."

"Then I'll do it," said the Little Red Hen. And that's just what she did.

"Who wants to eat this bread?" the Little Red Hen asked when the bread was ready.

"Honk honk! I do," said the Goose, drooling in the dirt. "I'm really hungry."

"Quack quack! I do," said the Duck, sniffing the sweet aroma. "It smells great."

"I'm sure you do, you lazy pair!" said the Little Red Hen. "But I did all the work, and I think I'll enjoy this myself with my family." Then she broke the bread into little bits and shared it with her chicks.

"Cluck cluck cluck!" It sure was delicious!

Peter Piper picked a peck of pickled peppers.

A peck of pickled peppers Peter Piper picked.

If Peter Piper picked a peck of pickled peppers,

Where's the peck of pickled peppers Peter Piper picked?

picked
pickled peppers

Burgers and Unfries

Pretty basic—but I wanted a perfect version. So, I asked Jon, one of our designers, to try it out on his two sons. Kai loved them but not Kojin. Jon gently explained that Kai was born in the Year of the Tiger but Kojin (born in the Year of the Mouse) wasn't a meat eater. Thank goodness for the Macaroni and Cheese recipe that follows.

Burgers

1 lb ground turkey or beef
1/2 cup diced onion
1/4 cup ketchup
1/3 cup milk
1/2 cup bread crumbs (see page 94)
1 egg
1/4 teaspoon salt
1/8 teaspoon pepper
butter (for frying pan method)
4 hamburger rolls

1. Preheat the grill, broiler, or get out the frying pan.
2. In a large bowl, mix meat, onion, ketchup, milk, bread crumbs, egg, salt, and pepper. Divide and shape into four patties.
3. If you are frying, put a pat of butter into a large frying pan over medium-high heat.
4. Grill, broil, or fry about 5 minutes on each side, until meat is no longer pink in the middle.
5. Serve with tomato, onion, or lettuce on rolls—and, of course, unfries!

Serves 4

Unfries

1 1/2 lbs baking potatoes (3 large), peeled (or not) and cut into strips
1 tablespoon grated Parmesan cheese
1 tablespoon vegetable oil
1/4 teaspoon each salt, garlic powder, paprika, and pepper

1. Preheat oven to 450°F.
2. Combine all ingredients in a bowl. Arrange on a baking sheet.
3. Bake 25 minutes or until brown. Serve with burgers and ketchup.

Serves 4

Macaroni and Cheese

Kids who don't like macaroni and cheese are few and far between. Make them happy with this simple dish or the slightly "jazzed up" macaroni casserole.

6 plus 2 tablespoons butter
1/4 cup plus 2 teaspoons all-purpose flour
3 cups milk
1 1/2 teaspoons dry mustard
1/8 teaspoon cayenne
salt and pepper to taste
1 lb elbow macaroni
3 cups coarsely grated extra sharp
    cheddar cheese (about 12 oz)
1 plus 1/3 cups grated Parmesan
    cheese (about 4 oz)
1 cup bread crumbs (you can use
    cornflakes, matzoh, or saltines,
    crushed in a plastic sandwich bag)

1. In a saucepan, melt 6 tablespoons butter over medium-low heat. Mix in flour and whisk until smooth and bubbly but not brown, about 3 minutes. Continue whisking as you slowly stir in the milk and bring to a gentle boil. Add mustard, cayenne and salt and pepper. Whisk for 5 minutes. Simmer, stirring occasionally, until sauce is thick, about 2 minutes.
2. Cook macaroni in a pot of boiling water for 7 to 8 minutes. Drain.
3. In a bowl combine macaroni, sauce, cheddar cheese, and 1 cup of Parmesan cheese and serve.

Macaroni Casserole

1. Preheat oven to 350°F and butter a 3- to 4-quart casserole dish.
2. Follow steps 1 to 3 above, then pour mixture into the buttered dish.
3. In a bowl, combine bread crumbs, 1 tablespoon of soft butter, and 1/3 cup of Parmesan. Mix well, making sure the butter is spread throughout. Sprinkle mixture on top of casserole and bake 25 to 30 minutes.

Serves 6 to 8

Franco (my guy) always ate what he made for his son Jay, and this is "guy" food at its easiest and best.

Quick and Easy Tacos

2 to 3 lbs ground turkey or beef
1 package taco seasoning
10 "folded", ready-to-fill taco shells,
  warmed

Toppings:
2 cups cheddar cheese (shredded)
1 small container sour cream
1 tomato (chopped)
1/2 head iceberg lettuce (shredded)
1 jar mild or medium salsa

1. In a large frying pan over medium-high heat, cook the meat until fully browned.
2. Follow the directions on the back of the taco seasoning mix. Add to meat and simmer until seasoned.
3. Put the toppings and meat into separate bowls. Let the kids fill their own tacos, meat first.

Serves 10

Tuna Melt

1 can (6-oz) tuna, drained
2 tablespoons mayonnaise
2 tablespoons butter
4 slices white or sourdough bread
2 slices cheddar cheese

1. Mix tuna and mayonnaise. Heat in microwave for 40 seconds on high.
2. In a small frying pan over medium heat, melt 1/2 tablespoon butter. Place a slice of bread in pan with a slice of the cheddar cheese on top. Cover pan until the cheese melts and the bread is lightly toasted.
3. Put 1/2 of the tuna on top of the cheese and another slice of bread on top. Add 1/2 tablespoon butter, turn and fry on other side. Remove from heat.
4. Repeat for second tuna melt.

Serves 2

The Brave Little Tailor

nce upon a time, in a village at the edge of the forest, a little tailor was sewing a coat for a customer. He was so focused on his work that he forgot to eat his lunch, and by late afternoon he felt starved.

"Strawberry jam for sale!" came a call from the window. "It's the sweetest jam around!"

"Yum," said the tailor, laying down the unfinished coat. "I'd like one jar, please."

He paid for the jam, spread it on a roll, and set it on the counter. "I'll finish the sleeves before eating," he said to himself. "Otherwise, the coat might get sticky."

By the time he finished the sleeves, he was so hungry his stomach was growling like a lion. He went to get the jam-covered roll but was too late—for there, buzzing and squirming in the jam, were seven hungry flies.

Instantly, the tailor raised his hand and slammed it on the flies. What a mess!

When he lifted his sticky hand, he counted: one, two, three,

The Brave Little Tailor

four, five, six, seven flies. They were all dead.

"Seven in one blow!" the little tailor said, impressed with himself. After eating a plain roll, he made himself a cloth belt and, in red thread, embroidered SEVEN IN ONE BLOW across the front. He put it on and admired himself in the mirror.

"I'm much too brave to be a tailor," he said. Then he locked his door and set off to find an adventure. The little tailor had walked less than a mile when one of the king's messengers stopped him by the side of the road.

"Seven in one blow!" the messenger said, staring at the tailor's belt. "I must bring you to the king." And so he did.

"Seven in one blow!" cried the king, as the little tailor stood before him. "Do you suppose you could get rid of the two evil giants that have been threatening the villagers?"

"I suppose so," said the little tailor. "I got rid of seven in one blow—and that's the truth."

The king gave him a sword and sent him into the forest.

The little tailor hadn't gone very far when he heard: *BOOM!*

The Brave Little Tailor

BOOM! BOOM! BOOM! The giants were coming!

Needing time to think, the little tailor scampered up an oak tree and peered out from the branches. The giants sure were ugly, especially when they yawned. One had no teeth and the other only one eye. When the giants reached the foot of the oak tree, they lay down for a nap.

Quietly, the little tailor picked up a pinecone and dropped it— *PLUNK*—onto the toothless giant's nose.

"Stop it!" the toothless giant growled, glaring at his partner.

"Stop what?" asked the one-eyed giant.

The little tailor dropped another pinecone on the toothless giant's nose—*PLUNK!*

"Stop *that!*" the toothless giant roared. He shoved the one-eyed giant, and soon the two of them were engaged in a terrible fight that made the whole forest tremble. Finally, each giant ripped a tree out of the earth—not the tree the tailor was in—and whacked each other until they were both knocked senseless.

"Marvelous work!" cried the king when the little tailor returned, for he had heard the good news. "I shall give you a reward; but first, do you suppose you could get rid of the ferocious unicorn that's been scaring the villagers?"

"I suppose so," said the little tailor. "I got rid of two evil giants and seven in one blow—and that's the truth."

The Brave Little Tailor

So once again, the little tailor set off for the woods. Before long, he heard: *BA-DRUMP! BA-DRUMP!* The unicorn was coming! Like all unicorns, this one had the head and body of a horse, the hind legs of a stag, the tail of a lion, and a horn in the center of its forehead. But unlike most unicorns, which are beautiful and gentle, this one was ferocious and had an exceptionally sharp horn—now pointed directly at the little tailor!

With no time to think and no time to climb a tree, the little tailor fainted to the ground, so instead of running into the little tailor, the unicorn charged—*BOING*—right into a tree. His horn stuck deep into the trunk.

"Now you shall have two rewards!" the king exclaimed. "But first, do you suppose you could get rid of the vicious wild boar that has been seen prowling around the villagers' homes?"

"I suppose so," said the little tailor. "I got rid of a ferocious unicorn, two evil giants, and seven in one blow—and that's the truth."

So a third time the little tailor went back to the woods. He'd gone less than two steps when he heard: *SNORT, SNORT!* The wild boar was coming! And it was the meanest beast the tailor had ever seen.

"Yikes!" the little tailor cried, and ran as fast as his little legs would carry him. The wild boar followed right behind, nipping at

The Brave Little Tailor

his heels. The little tailor saw a hut and ran into it. But before he could slam the door, the wild boar came in behind him. The little tailor saw a little window and climbed through it. Then he hurried around to the front and locked the door. Luckily, the wild boar was too large to fit through the little window.

"Now you shall have three rewards!" cried the king. "But first, do you suppose you could get rid of a dragon that—"

"I'm *sure* I could," said the little tailor, "whatever it is. I got rid of a vicious wild boar, a ferocious unicorn, two evil giants, and seven in one blow—and that's the truth. But if you don't mind, I'd like to take my reward and go home. I have some work to finish."

So the exhausted little tailor carried three bags of gold back to his shop. Before getting back to his sewing, he took off the belt that said SEVEN IN ONE BLOW and hung it in the back of his closet. "From now on, I think I'll stay home," he said to himself. Then he curled up on his bed and took a long, peaceful nap.

And to this day, the dragon the king wanted him to get rid of is still roaming around in the woods.

Song to Be Sung by the Father of Infant Female Children

by Ogden Nash

My heart leaps up when I behold
A rainbow in the sky;
Contrariwise, my blood runs cold
When little boys go by.
For little boys as little boys,
No special hate I carry,
But now and then they grow to men,
And when they do, they marry.
No matter how they tarry,
Eventually they marry.
And, swine among the pearls,
They marry little girls....

Oh, somewhere he bubbles bubbles of milk,
And quietly sucks his thumbs.
His cheeks are roses painted on silk,
And his teeth are tucked in his gums.

But alas the teeth will begin to grow,
And the bubbles will cease to bubble;
Given a score of years or so,
The roses will turn to stubble.
He'll sell a bond, or he'll write a book,
And his eyes will get that acquisitive look,
And raging and ravenous for the kill,
He'll boldly ask for the hand of Jill.
This infant whose middle
Is diapered still
Will want to marry My daughter Jill.

Oh sweet be his slumber and moist his middle!
My dreams, I fear, are infanticiddle.
A fig for embryo Lohengrins!
I'll open all his safety pins,
I'll pepper his powder, and salt his bottle,
And give him readings from Aristotle.
Sand for his spinach I'll gladly bring,
And Tabasco sauce for his teething ring.
Then perhaps he'll struggle through fire and water
To marry somebody else's daughter.

Georgy Porgy

Georgy Porgy,
pudding and pie,

Kissed the girls and
made them cry.

When the boys
came out to play,

Georgy Porgy ran away.

Froggy Went a-Courtin'

Frog - gie went a - court - in' and he did ride, a

huh, a huh.

Frog - gie went a - court - in' and he did ride, a

sword and pis - tol by his side, a

Froggy Went a-Courtin'

huh. a huh. Well, he

rode down to Miss Mous - e's door, a

huh, a huh. Well, he rode down to Miss

Mous - e's door, where he had of - ten

been be - fore, a huh, a huh.

Froggy Went a-Courtin'

3. He took Miss Mousie on his knee,
   a-huh, a-huh,
   He took Miss Mousie on his knee,
   Said, "Miss Mousie will you marry
   me?" A-huh, a-huh.

4. "I'll have to ask my Uncle Rat, etc.
   See what he will say to that," etc.

5. "Without my Uncle Rat's consent,
   I would not marry the President."

6. Well, Uncle Rat laughed and shook
   his sides,
   To think his niece would be a bride.

7. Well, Uncle Rat rode off to town
   To buy his niece a wedding gown.

8. "Where will the wedding supper be?"
   "Way down yonder in a hollow tree."

9. "What will the wedding supper be?"
   "A fried mosquito and a roasted flea."

10. First to come in were two little ants,
    Fixing around to have a dance.

11. Next to come in was a bumble bee,
    Bouncing a fiddle on his knee.

12. Next to come in was a fat sassy lad,
    Thinks himself as big as his dad.

13. Thinks himself a man indeed,
    Because he chews the tobacco weed.

14. And next to come in was a big tomcat,
    He swallowed the frog and the mouse
    and the rat.

15. Next to come in was a big old snake,
    He chased the party into the lake.

16. There's bread and honey on the shelf,
    If you want anymore just sing it yourself.

Daisy, Daisy

While the goddesses of ancient Greece wore daisy chains, divinity is not a prerequisite to wearing these beautiful strings of flowers. Take your child to an open field to pick fresh daisies. Use some to make daisy chains for the head or neck. Teach your child how to say "He/she loves me, He/she loves me not" with the petals. Then take some home to press and dry for making special art for mom.

DAISY CHAINS
daisies

1. Break the stems so that they are about an inch long.
2. Using your fingernail, make a small slit near the middle of the stem.
3. Thread the stem of the second daisy through the slit of the first. The head of the second flower should rest against the stem of the first.
4. Make a slit on the second flower and thread a third flower through. Continue threading daisies until you run out of daisies or the chain reaches the desired length.
5. Tie the stems on each end together to close your chain.

PRESSED DAISIES
daisies, white drawing paper, heavy books, glue, construction paper or stationery, crayons

1. Place freshly picked daisies between two sheets of drawing paper. Press between the pages of a heavy book. Place more books on top. Set in a warm, dry place for about a week.
2. Carefully remove the flowers from the paper.
3. Let your child paste onto construction paper and complete the scene with crayons. Or let your child glue daisies to the edges of stationery for pretty floral notes for their favorite people.

Knock knock!

Knock Knock!

Who's there?

Boo.

Boo who?

What's the matter?

Don't cry!

Knock Knock!

Who's there?

Atch.

Atch who?

God bless you! Are you
getting a cold?

Knock Knock!

Who's there?

Cows.

Cows who?

Cows don't go who.

Cows go moo!

Knock Knock!

Who's there?

You.

You who?

Are you calling me?

Knock Knock?
> *Who's there?*

Ya.
> *Ya who?*

Yahoo? Are you
a cowboy?

Knock Knock!
> *Who's there?*

A little old lady.
> *A little old lady who?*

I didn't know
you can yodel.

Knock Knock!
> *Who's there?*

Banana.
> *Banana who?*

Knock Knock!
> *Who's there?*

Banana.
> *Banana who?*

Knock Knock!
> *Who's there?*

Orange.
> *Orange who?*

Orange you glad I
didn't say banana?

Who's there?

Zebra Question
by Shel Silverstein

I asked the zebra,
Are you black with white stripes?
Or white with black stripes?
And the zebra asked me,
Are you good with bad habits?
Or are you bad with good habits?
Are you noisy with quiet times?
Or are you quiet with noisy times?
Are you happy with some sad days?
Or are you sad with some happy days?
Are you neat with some sloppy ways?
Or are you sloppy with some neat ways?
And on and on and on and on
And on and on he went.
I'll never ask a zebra
About stripes
Again.

Pony Man

Words and Music by Gordon Lightfoot

When it's mid-night on the mead-ow and the

cats are in the shed   *piano*   And the

riv-er tells a sto-ry at the win-dow by my

bed,   *piano*   If you lis-ten ver-y

Pony Man

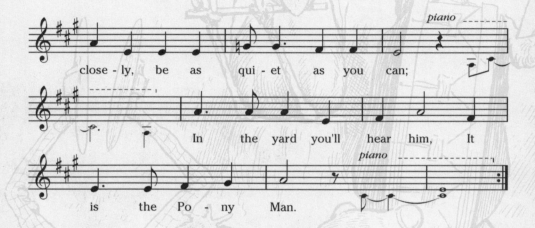

close - ly,   be   as   qui - et   as   you   can;

In   the   yard   you'll   hear   him,   It

is   the   Po - ny   Man.

Pony Man

2. We're always there to greet him
When he tumbles into town.
He leads a string of ponies
Some are white and some are brown.
And they never seem to kick or bite,
They only want to play.
They live on candy apples
Instead of oats and hay.

3. And when we are assembled
He gives a soft command.
And we climb aboard our ponies
As in a row they stand.
Then down the road we gallop
And across the fields we fly.
And soon we all go sailing off
Into the midnight sky.

4. And as we gaily rock along
Beside a ripplin' sea,
There's Tom and Dick and Sally
And Mary Jo and me
And the Pony Man is leading
'Cause he's travelled here before
And he gives a whoop and holler
At Mister Moon's front door.

5. And then we stop to rest awhile
Where the soda river glides,
Up to the slip comes a pirate ship
To take us for a ride.
And the Pony Man's the captain
And the children are the crew.
And we go in search of treasure
And laugh the whole night through.

6. And when the hold is filled with gold
And the sails begin to strain,
And the deck's piled high with apple pie
We head for port again.
Then down the whirling star case
So swift our ponies fly.
And we're safely in our beds again
When sunbeams kiss the sky.

7. *Repeat first verse*.

Knight for a Day

Children like to try on different hats—they like to be kings one day and knights the next. Here is an easy paper hat that can serve as a costume when imaginations take over. Add a broomstick horse and a crafty sword, and your child can defend his or her imaginary kingdom for hours.

PAPER HAT
11 x 17-inch sheet of paper

1. Fold the paper in half to 8$\frac{1}{2}$ x 11 inches.
2. With the creased side at the top, fold the two top corners to meet in the middle so that the paper looks like the top of a giant arrow.
3. There should be a rectangular portion underneath the triangular portion of your arrow-top. Fold up one rectangular flap and crease at the bottom of the triangle. Turn over and repeat with the other flap.
4. Decorate with crayons or glue on a feather or a leaf.

PAPER SWORD
2 empty paper towel rolls, masking tape, scissors, aluminum foil

1. Flatten the paper towel rolls. Tape edges closed to hold flattened shape.
2. Tape the ends of two rolls together.
3. Trim off two corners on one end to create a point on the sword. Tape edges together.
4. Wrap the sword with aluminum foil to make a steely blade!

BROOMSTICK HORSE
small broomstick, white athletic sock, tissue, rubber band, marker, scissor, paper, glue, yarn

1. Stuff the foot portion of the sock with tissue.
2. Pull the tube portion over the non-bristle end of the broomstick and secure with a rubber band. The sock should now look something like a horse's head.
3. Decorate the head with the marker, creating eyes, nose, and mouth. You can also glue on paper ears and a yarn mane.

Puss in Boots

Once upon a time, a miller died and left his eldest son a mill, his second son a donkey, and his third son a cat.

"What a useless cat," the third son said, watching it sleep in the grass. "All it does is sleep, sleep, *sleep*! At least my brothers can earn a living with a mill and a donkey. But who ever heard of earning a living with a cat? I might as well just eat it and be full for a day!"

"No way!" the cat exclaimed, springing to its feet. "Fetch me a pair of boots and a sack, Master, and I'll see that you have great riches in no time."

The young man stared at the cat, for he had never heard it speak.

"The name is Puss," the cat said. "And I wear size six in a boot."

The young man did as he was asked and was impressed at how charming Puss looked in his shiny new boots.

Quick as a flash, Puss scampered into the woods, caught a rabbit, and stuffed it into his sack. Then he went to the palace and presented it to the king. "Sire, the Marquis of Carabas sends you this fine rabbit," he announced.

Though the king had never heard of the Marquis of Carabas

(Puss had made him up), he did love rabbit. "Please thank the Marquis," he said, handing Puss a gold coin.

Over the next few days, Puss brought the king a quail, a trout, and a pheasant. "Be sure to thank the Marquis," the king said each time, handing Puss a gold coin.

Meanwhile back at the cottage, which they had bought with two gold coins, the young man was amused. "Me? The Marquis of Carabas?" he said, chuckling. But he was grateful for the gold.

One morning, Puss heard that the king and his pretty daughter would be going out for a drive along the river. "Hurry, Master!" he cried. "Jump in the river and act like you're drowning."

By the time the king's carriage rolled toward the river, the young man was splashing and spluttering in the water.

"Help!" Puss cried, waving in front of the carriage. "The Marquis of Carabas is drowning! Thieves stole his clothes!" (Puss had really hidden them under a rock.)

Recognizing Puss, the king shouted orders to his men: "Rescue the Marquis at once! Send for some fine new clothes."

Before long, the young man was dressed in satins and silks. The king was impressed by how handsome he looked—but not as impressed as the princess. "Join us on our drive," she said shyly, making room on the seat. The young man climbed into the carriage and found the princess to be quite charming.

Puss in Boots

Puss dashed ahead and came to an orchard. "When the king asks," he said to the harvesters, "tell him this orchard belongs to the Marquis of Carabas."

"Okay," the harvesters said.

Minutes later, when the king asked who the orchard belonged to, the harvesters answered, "The Marquis of Carabas." The king raised an eyebrow.

By then, Puss was up ahead, giving orders to a group of fishermen.

"Who owns these boats?" the king called out when the carriage rolled by the dock.

"The Marquis of Carabas," answered the fishermen. The king beamed at the young man sitting next to his daughter.

Soon Puss came to an ogre's castle that was every bit as elegant as the king's palace. The ogre also owned all the surrounding land.

"Who have we here?" the ogre sneered, inspecting Puss from head to boot tip.

"The name is Puss, and I'm here to find out if the rumors are true. Can you really turn yourself into a lion?"

"Grrr!" roared the ogre, and he instantly became a ferocious lion.

"Incr-r-redible," Puss said, trembling. He was relieved when the ogre became himself again. "But I'll bet you couldn't turn yourself into a tiny mouse."

Puss in Boots

"Oh yeah?" the ogre sneered. Instantly, a tiny mouse stood in his place. Quick as a flash, Puss gobbled him up.

By the time the king's carriage arrived at the castle, Puss was standing proudly at the front gate. "Welcome, Sire, to the home of the Marquis of Carabas!"

"What a magnificent home!" the king said admiringly.

"Why thank you," said the young man, suddenly feeling like a real Marquis. "Won't you come in?"

"Not until you agree to marry me," the princess said, blushing.

"Splendid idea!" said the king, overjoyed. "I'd be honored to have the Marquis of Carabas as my son-in-law."

"I'd be honored to marry your daughter," said the Marquis, taking the princess's hand.

They were married the next day. The Marquis's brothers, who came as guests, were amazed at their brother's success.

"I have the cat to thank," the Marquis of Carabas said, smiling proudly at Puss. "A mill and a donkey are nice, but a cat in boots—now, that's a real a treasure!"

After the ceremony, the Marquis appointed Puss Lord of the Castle and proclaimed him the Smartest Cat in the Land. And Puss spent the rest of his days sleeping to his heart's content, without fear of being eaten by man or beast.

Pussy-Cat
and
Queen

"Pussy-cat, pussy-cat,
  Where have you been?"

"I've been to London
  To look at the Queen."

"Pussy-cat, pussy-cat,
  What did you there?"

"I frightened a little mouse
  Under the chair."

Transformations

by Tadeusz Rózewicz
Translated by Czeslaw Milosz

My little son enters
the room and says
"you are a vulture
I am a mouse"

I put away my book
wings and claws
grow out of me

their ominous shadows
race on the walls
I am a vulture
he is a mouse

"you are a wolf
I am a goat"
I walk around the table
and am a wolf
windowpanes gleam
like fangs
in the dark
while he runs to his mother
safe
his head hidden in the
    warmth of her dress

Easy Magic

All kids think their fathers have superpowers—prove them right while they still believe in magic. The following magic tricks are easy and safe, but they will require some practicing. The disappearing coin trick has been around forever and does not cease to amaze. The heads or tails trick is a great one to bet on. Tell your child that he or she has to clean up or eat tons of vegetables if you can guess heads or tails correctly—and you always will.

COIN-SWALLOWING ELBOW
a coin and some flair

1. Show your audience the coin in your right hand. Bend your left elbow, placing your left hand on the back of your neck. With your right hand, rub the coin vigorously back and forth into the elbow. After some time, say that the trick works better with the other hand and drop the coin on the table.
2. Pick the coin up with your right hand, and *pretend* to quickly put it into the left hand. Then start rubbing the imaginary coin into the right elbow, while pressing the coin in your right hand into the back of your neck or under your shirt collar.

3. Expose both empty hands with a grand *"ta da!"*

HEADS OR TAILS?
quarter, improved upon

1. Using a hammer and a nail, make a nick on one side of a quarter. Note what side you make this on.
2. Practice dropping the quarter on a table—it will make a duller sound when it lands on the side with the nick. Memorize the sound!
3. Tell your child you can guess heads or tails correctly every time. Let your child spin the quarter or toss it over the table. Listen for the difference and amaze your child.

Marshmallow Fun

Children love to build things, play with their food, and eat sweets, so you can imagine how much fun they'll have with these activities. Learning to juggle with marshmallows is safe and a whole bag of fun. If juggling on a relatively clean surface, the five-second rule applies—food on the floor for no more than five seconds can still be eaten!

MARSHMALLOW CONSTRUCTION

bag of marshmallows, toothpicks, clean surface

1. Use toothpicks to connect marshmallows together.
2. Build a marshmallow family, a tower, or simply the longest chain of marshmallows imagined.
3. When tired of building, eat.

CHILD-PROOF JUGGLING

bag of large marshmallows

1. Take one marshmallow and practice throwing it in a low arc from one hand to the other. Keep practicing until you can transfer the marshmallow from one hand to the other keeping the same low arc, with few mistakes.
2. Hold a marshmallow in each hand. Throw one marshmallow in a low arc to the other hand. As the first marshmallow starts to drop, throw the second marshmallow in a low arc to the other hand. Practice until you have the rhythm.
3. Add the third marshmallow to the mix. Hold two marshmallows in one hand and one marshmallow in the other. Using the hand holding two marshmallows, throw one marshmallow in a low arc to the other hand. As the first marshmallow reaches the top of the arc, throw the marshmallow in the other hand, again in a low arc. Just as the second marshmallow reaches the top of the arc and the first marshmallow lands in your hand, throw the last marshmallow.
4. Remember the five-second rule.

The Emperor's New Clothes

nce upon a time there lived an emperor who loved clothes. The only reason he ever went to the theater, to banquets, or on strolls was to show off his latest outfit. He spent more time trying on his clothes and standing in front of the mirror than he did taking care of his country. He had an outfit for every hour of the day!

One day, two men—one tall and thin like a pencil, the other short and squat like a bullfrog—arrived at the palace. They said they were weavers, though they were really swindlers, people who trick other people.

"We can weave a golden fabric more beautiful and exquisite than any you can imagine," said the taller swindler.

"And most amazing of all," said the shorter swindler, "the fabric is invisible to anyone stupid. Only smart people can see it."

"Hmm," the Emperor said, scratching his chin. "A beautiful fabric only smart people can see? Make me a new outfit at once!" he demanded. He paid the swindlers a large sum and ordered that a weaving room be prepared.

The Emperor's New Clothes

Two great looms and a case of golden thread were ordered, and soon the swindlers got to work—*pretending* to weave the fine fabrics. They were really weaving nothing at all and had stuffed the golden thread into their bags.

For the next three days, the swindlers pretended to slave away at the empty looms while the impatient Emperor tried to be patient. "I can't take it any more!" he finally shouted. "I must have a peek at the new fabric." But as he strutted toward the door of the weaving room, he began to feel nervous.

"What if *I* can't see the fabric?" he thought. "After all, it's a special material that only smart, interesting people can see." He knew he was smart and interesting—but was he smart and interesting *enough* to see the fabric? By now, everyone in town had heard about the magical powers of the fabric and was anxious to find out which of their neighbors could see it and which of them couldn't. If a rumor got around that the Emperor couldn't see it, he'd be the laughingstock of the town. Just to be safe, the Emperor sent his most reliable adviser to see it first.

"Have you ever seen such lovely fabric?" the taller swindler asked the adviser as he

The Emperor's New Clothes

pretended to hold up a section.

"I, I'm speechless," the adviser said, reaching for his glasses. But even with his glasses, he couldn't see a thing.

"I must be stupid!" the adviser thought with surprise. "But if the Emperor finds out, I'll lose my job." He forced a smile and lied. "It's absolutely fabulous, and the patterns are charming." Then he hurried off to tell the Emperor the exact same thing.

After another week, the Emperor became fidgety. "I've ordered two new cases of golden thread," he said to his oldest and wisest lord. "They must be near done." But the Emperor was still a bit hesitant to check on the weavers himself. He sent the lord instead.

"I'll bet you've never seen such magnificent beauty," the shorter swindler said to the lord, pretending to stroke the fine fabric.

"I can't see a thing," the lord thought to himself, though he knew he was no fool. "But if the Emperor finds out I'll lose my job." So, the lord praised the swindlers' work. "It's marvelously elegant," he lied. Then he hurried off to tell the Emperor the exact same thing.

Soon, the Emperor couldn't bear the suspense any longer. He gathered all the advisers, lords, and ladies of the court together and led them to the weaving room.

"My lords and ladies, have you ever seen such a remarkable

design?" said the taller swindler.

"Or such truly original colors?" said the shorter swindler.

The Emperor was horrified! He couldn't see a thing.

"I mustn't let anyone know that I'm stupid," he thought. "Otherwise, I'll be tossed off the throne—maybe even out of the country!" The advisers, lords, and ladies of the court complimented the swindlers on their wonderful work. (They were pretending, of course!)

"Superb!" the Emperor said. "I'll be honored to wear them in the great parade." The parade was to take place the following day. Since everyone else could see the fabric, he'd just have to trust them. He felt sure it would impress the townspeople as well—at least the smart, interesting ones.

The swindlers burned candles all that night so everyone would think they were working hard to finish up the Emperor's new clothes. Early the next morning, the advisers, lords, and ladies of the court escorted the Emperor to the weaving room.

"Charming! Delightful!" everyone cried as the swindlers held up each garment.

The Emperor's New Clothes

But no one saw a thing!

"We're thrilled you're pleased, Your Majesty," the swindlers said as the Emperor undressed. Then they pretended to help him dress in his pretend new clothes. When they were finished, the Emperor stood proudly in his plain old underwear.

The parade soon began.

"Look at those magnificent clothes!" the townspeople cried. "What lovely colors and patterns!" Nobody dared to admit they couldn't see the new clothes at all—except for the children.

"But he has nothing on but his underwear!" said a giggling boy.

"Papa, his legs are as hairy as yours!" said a giggling girl.

"Mama, look at the king's big belly!" said another boy, who puffed out his own belly to imitate the Emperor.

"I see the Emperor's belly button, I see the Emperor's belly button," a group of children began to chant.

The children's giggles and chants made too much sense to be ignored by the adults, who also began to point and laugh.

The poor Emperor was so embarrassed he ran straight home, one hand over his chest and the other over his belly button. And from that day forth, he always wore plain, gray suits.

The Lion and

The Lion and
the Unicorn were
fighting for
the crown,

The Lion beat
the Unicorn all
around the town.

the Unicorn

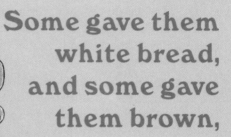

Some gave them
white bread,
and some gave
them brown,

Some gave them
plum-cake, and
sent them out of town.

The Same River Twice

Chris Offutt

My son is three months old and on my back, strapped in a red harness. Today is the first day of spring, his first visit to the woods. His chubby legs bounce against my back. Seventeen years have elapsed since the last locust outbreak and the forest floor is full of finger-size holes. The earth has given the insects to light. Their drone rises and falls around us like distant chain saws. Rita is home, grateful for some time alone. Our son sleeps between us in the bed, and at night I arrange myself in order to hold his hand.

Flocks of starlings migrate along the river. The softwoods bud, the hardwoods wait. My family and I talk more often on the phone. Dad inquires about the "son of my son," I ask him what he wants the kid to call him. "Grandfather," he says. "That way he'll always know there's someone grander than his father.

My mother wants to know who he resembles and I tell her he looks like himself, realizing later that the same phrase is used to describe a corpse lying in state. We live far away from them. I grew up not seeing my grandparents and have always regretted the loss. Now it would seem the pattern repeats.

The load on my back weighs nothing and everything. I stop to shift him, and feel a vine on my leg, around my boot. It is a tiny

The Same River Twice

garter snake. Behind its head is a yellow stripe the size of a wedding ring. I pick it up gently, knowing that children accidentally kill them through gleeful handling. I turn my head to my son and hold the snake over my shoulder. His little fingers float toward it, pull back.

The river is high from flood to the north. Rita and I are always sleepy. Six weeks after the birth, our doctor sanctioned making love, but our son interrupted us the first few times. It

seemed fitting somehow and I didn't mind the halt. I was worried that Rita would feel different to me, that birth had transformed her passage. Her breasts had already become utilitarian, functioning independent of aesthetics. Making love to a maiden is one thing, to a mother quite another. When our son slept, Rita and I molded together, pressing as much flesh against each other as possible. My fears shed as easily as autumn leaves in rain. Nothing had changed except everything.

I come to a downed tree and remove the pack containing my son. The pack has an aluminum bar that folds forward so it can stand alone. It is bigger than him and he slumps sideways, listing like a trawler. I straighten him and he slides the other way. No matter how I try, he cannot sit straight, but his eyes the color of mine never leave my face. I sit cross-legged before

The Same River Twice

him. The woods are heavy around us. The equinox signals the beginning of life and crop, of nesting birds and mating animals. I want to explain everything. I want to tell him what to do, and more important, what not to do. I give him a leaf which he calmly tastes. He can't learn from my mistakes, only from his own.

I think of all the things I want to tell him, and say nothing. According to my father, I come from a long line of bad fathers, improving with each generation. The birth of my son has made me a middle-man, nearer to death and to life, closer to my father. With courage and work, my son will become an adult one day. Amid the trees and birds, I realize that despite the obstacles I set myself, I have somehow become one myself.

I press my forehead to the forehead of my son. His tiny brow is warm. I can see his fontanel pulsing with life. Daddy loves you, is all I can think to say. Like all sons before him, he says nothing. The woods enclose us like a tent. The river flows beside us and touching it means touching the sea.

■

There is no heavier burden than potential.

—Charlie Brown

King Midas

nce upon a time, there was a very rich king named Midas, who loved gold. His favorite thing to do was to count his gold.

"One golden flute, two golden duckies, three golden bicycles…"

The king had a daughter named Zoe. Sometimes Zoe would interrupt King Midas's counting.

"Daddy," said Zoe. "Let's play hide-and-seek in the rose garden."

"When I'm done, sweetie," the king would say—and then forget his promise. Not that he didn't love his beautiful daughter, but counting his gold kept him busy, busy, busy. And the more he counted, the more he wanted.

One day, King Midas was counting his gold as usual: "thirty-nine golden walruses, forty golden pickles—"

Suddenly a voice interrupted him.

"You sure are rich!" said the voice.

"Not rich enough," King Midas said, as a strange man stepped out from the shadows. "Anyway, who are you?"

"That's not important," said the man. "I'm here to grant you

King Midas

one wish. You can think about—"

"I *know* what I want!" said the king, his eyes brightening. "I love gold. I want everything I touch to turn to gold!"

"Are you sure?" asked the stranger.

"Sure I'm sure," said King Midas. "Gold makes me happy, happy, happy!"

"OK," said the stranger. "Tomorrow morning you'll have the golden touch."

The next morning, King Midas woke up and turned off his alarm clock—and, instantly, it turned to gold! So did his sheets and blankets, rug and curtains, and toothbrush and toothpaste!

"Yippee!" King Midas shouted as he raced down the royal staircase—which instantly turned to gold. Bubbling with excitement, he went to the rose garden to pick a bouquet for the breakfast room. He plucked a perfect rose from its stem and held it close to his nose to take in its fragrance. But he couldn't smell a thing—for it had turned to gold. So did every rose he touched.

"I'll have to remember to sniff them without touching," he thought with disappointment.

Meow!

"Oops!" King Midas said, scooping up his favorite cat. "I didn't see you there, Fuzzball."

King Midas

But instead of feeling the cat's warm, snuggly fur, he felt hard, cold gold. A tear ran down his face, changing to gold before it hit the stone path. For the cat had always been a great companion.

When the king arrived at breakfast he popped a grape into his mouth—and nearly broke a tooth! For the grape had changed into gold. So did a bagel, a piece of bacon, and a glass of orange juice.

"I CAN'T STAND THIS ANYMORE!" the king finally roared.

"Stand what?" Zoe asked, rushing into the room. When she saw her father crying, she went to comfort him.

"Noooo!" the king shouted, trying to stop his daughter from touching him. But he was too late.

"My precious Zoe!" King Midas wailed, hugging the hard, gold statue that only seconds before had been his lovely daughter. "You're worth more to me than all the gold in the world!"

"I thought the golden touch would make you happy, happy, happy," said a familiar voice.

Through golden tears, King Midas made out the shape of the stranger who had granted him his wish.

"Well, it didn't," the king sobbed. "Getting my wonderful daughter back will make me happy, and my furry cat, and my sweet-smelling roses."

"Very well," said the stranger. "But it will cost you all the gold you have."

King Midas

"Fine!" said King Midas. "Gold just makes me miserable, miserable, miserable!"

"Then wash your hands in the nearest brook," the stranger said, "and fill a jug with water. Take it back to the palace and sprinkle it on everything you changed to gold. Soon—"

But before the stranger could finish, King Midas was already fetching the water.

"It works!" King Midas shouted, when he saw the jug change from gold to clay. He raced back to the palace and sprinkled water over the golden statue.

"What are you doing, Daddy?" Zoe asked, wiping her wet face on her sleeve. (She had no idea what had happened to her.)

"Having fun!" King Midas shouted, as he gleefully sprinkled the golden cat—which suddenly came back to life. Meow!

"Cool!" Zoe exclaimed. "Can I try it?"

The king handed the jug to Zoe. She sprinkled a golden rose—which instantly became red again, its fragrance sweeter than ever!

King Midas and Zoe sprinkled and sprinkled until everything King Midas's golden touch had changed was back to normal. Then they moved to a log cabin at the edge of a forest, played hide-and-seek, and lived happily ever after.

The Crooked

There was a crooked man, and
    he went a crooked mile,

He found a crooked sixpence
    beside a crooked stile;

He bought a crooked cat, which
    caught a crooked mouse,

And they all lived together
    in a little crooked house.

Sixpence

The Wonder of Being Dad . . . Again

Glenn T. Stanton

I just became a father again . . . for the fifth time with the birth of our daughter Isabel Lee.

As I reflect on Isabel's birth, I am struck by how *extraordinary* the experience remains. This birth was just as phenomenal as when our first child was born six years ago and as magical as each of the three in between.

The special drama of this pregnancy was watching our four curious kids anxiously anticipate every stage, from the pictures of the first ultra-sound, to the day we found out the sex (we always wanted to know as soon as we could, like kids who can't wait until Christmas!). They were excited about setting up the new nursery. They loved seeing mom getting big (but not THAT big, I reminded her to no comfort). And they all had a hand in adding to and narrowing down our list of names.

The big day was all planned. Initiated by my wife's increasing discomfort, I (half-kidding) asked our OB if we could schedule an inducement two weeks before the due date. To our amazement and delight, he pulled out his schedule book and asked, "How is the 12th for you guys?" Now we had a target date and we counted the minutes.

The Wonder of Being Dad . . . Again

But of all the special moments leading up to the event, the biggest was the fact that our doctor asked *me* if I wanted to deliver this child. It was one of the most male-affirming things I have ever done. I was "the man." My wife and I conceived this little person in soulful solitude and we brought her into the world in partnership. We were a team.

But my adventure in fatherhood is only beginning. With five kids, ages six and under (our twins helped us in that feat), I live life on the edge every day. And that is where the wonder of a new baby really lies, not only in conception and birth, but also in the real BIG event called life. Every new life does nothing less than change the course of history and the balance of the universe by its very existence. That's big stuff. I will be a key player in Isabel's life as she grows, along with her siblings, into the fullness of her humanity. And this doesn't happen by itself. As a male parent, I have a distinct and irreplaceable role in this process.

I will be there to provide them with the knowledge that men are dependable. I will be there to teach each of them (to the best of my ability) how a man cares for and loves a woman. I will strive to be the measure by which my four daughters choose their husbands and the model for my son when he becomes one. I will be there to teach them to love God and others with all their might. I will be there to perform one of the greatest tasks a man can do: I will be a dad to Isabel, Tess, Sophie, Schaeffer and Olivia.

■

Little Tom Tucker

Little Tom Tucker
    Sings for his supper.
What shall he eat?
    White bread and butter.
How will he cut it
    Without e'er a knife?
How will he be married
    Without e'er a wife?

Tennessee Corn Pone

Franco made it for his 4-year-old son Jay eighteen years ago. I ate a version of it with my friends Nancy and Geoff when my daughters babysat for their daughter Leland at about the same time. My whole family loves it. If you don't have time to finish the chili with the corn bread batter, serve the chili (sprinkled with cheddar cheese) with Corn Bread *(page 162)* and some green salad. (Then you can put the leftovers in a baking dish, pour some cornbread batter over the top; and do it properly the next day!)

2½ cups dried kidney beans soaked
   4 to 5 hours or, preferably, overnight,
   drained (or two 13½ -oz cans,
   drained and rinsed)
2 tablespoons olive oil
2 cups diced onions
6 minced garlic cloves
1 diced carrot
1 diced celery stalk
2 teaspoons each cumin, basil, chili
   powder, and salt
black pepper and cayenne, to taste
1 lb ground beef (optional)
1 diced bell pepper
1 cup V-8 juice
1 (14½ -oz) can tomatoes

3 tablespoons tomato paste
1 cup shredded cheddar cheese
   (optional)

1. If using dried beans, add water and the soaked beans to a large pot and bring to a boil. Turn heat down, partially cover, and simmer the beans, covered with water, for 1¼ hours. Drain.

2. Heat olive oil in a large skillet. Add onion, garlic, carrot, celery, and seasonings. Saute over medium heat for 5 minutes.

(continued)

Tennessee Corn Pone

Add ground beef, if desired, bell pepper, and saute until vegetables are soft and beef shows no pink.

3. Add vegetable mixture, V-8 juice, tomatoes, and tomato paste to the pot of beans. Simmer over very low heat, stirring occasionally, for 20 to 30 minutes.
4. While the chili is simmering, prepare the corn bread batter. Follow steps 1 to 3 in the corn bread recipe following.
5. Pour the chili into a baking pan, cover with the corn bread batter, and bake in a preheated 375°F oven for 25 minutes. Serve pone with green salad.
6. Alternatively, taste after step 3, sprinkle with cheddar cheese (you can also add a little finely chopped raw onion and bell pepper), and simply serve chili with green salad and corn bread.

Serves 6 to 8

Corn bread

1 1/4 cups unbleached white flour
3/4 cup corn meal
4 tablespoons sugar
5 teaspoons baking powder
3/4 teaspoon salt
1 egg
1 cup of milk or buttermilk
2 tablespoons melted butter
1/2 cup grated cheddar cheese (optional)

1. Preheat oven to 375°F.
2. In a mixing bowl, combine dry ingredients.
3. In another bowl, beat the egg with the milk, butter, and cheese. Add to the flour mixture and stir until smooth.
4. Butter a 9-inch pie plate, pour in batter, and bake for 30 minutes.
5. Serve cornbread hot with butter or cold with salad and chili.

Serves 6

Chicken Fingers

Clark's two little girls, Eve and Sylvia, love chicken fingers. These are such wonderful finger foods for children. Serve with Unfries *(page 93)* or Potato Pancakes *(page 165)* and steamed broccoli for a complete meal.

4 boneless, skinless chicken breasts
1 egg
3 tablespoons milk
1/4 cup grated Parmesan cheese
1 1/2 cups bread crumbs (see page 94)
salt and pepper to taste
parsley, thyme, or oregano (optional)
4 tablespoons butter

1. Slice chicken breasts into finger-sized strips.
2. In a bowl, mix together egg, milk, and cheese.
3. In another bowl, mix bread crumbs, salt and pepper, and dried herbs, if desired.
4. Drench the chicken slices in the egg mixture and then roll in the bread crumbs. Put on waxed paper.
5. Melt the butter in a large skillet and cook the chicken over medium-high heat. Do not overcrowd the chicken and cook in batches if necessary. You can dab a bit of butter onto the chicken as it cooks to make it extra crispy. Cook about 15 minutes, turning chicken strips as they brown. Remove and drain on paper towel.
6. Alternatively, you can bake the chicken in the oven at 425°F for 25 minutes, turning the pieces over midway.
7. Serve with dips like honey, honey mustard, and sweet and sour or barbecue sauce.
   Serves 4

Sloppy Joes

Oh, this is so messy and so good. My kids ate it over and over again. Their dad poured it over macaroni. He poured it over rice. He put in on English muffins and he served it on top of toast. He even got me to use it as a sauce for a lasagna I used to make with tomato sauce, ricotta, mozzarella, and Parmesan cheese. That was 25 years ago. Today in our little office of eight people (who between them have six little ones under five) it is Jacinta's husband Adam who makes this for four-year-old William.

2 tablespoons olive oil
2 onions, chopped
4 celery stalks, chopped
4 cloves crushed garlic
2 lbs lean ground beef
1 cup tomato sauce
3 tablespoons tomato paste
1/2 cup ketchup
1 teaspoon tabasco sauce
2 teaspoons Worcestershire sauce
salt and pepper to taste

1. Heat oil in large heavy skillet over low heat. Add the onion and celery and cook until soft and lightly browned.
2. Add the garlic and continue cooking 3 to 4 minutes.
3. Increase heat to medium high and add the ground beef. Cook about 10 to 12 minutes until meat is browned.
4. Lower heat to medium and add the tomato sauce, tomato paste, ketchup, tabasco, and Worcestershire sauce. Cook, stirring, about 15 to 30 minutes until the liquid is reduced and the mixture becomes thick.
5. Add salt and pepper to taste.

Serves 6 people

Potato Pancakes

My friend Marty is one of the great dads in this universe and I met his daughter Sasi when she was twelve. She was the only eccentric 12 year old I had ever known and she was an astonishing cook. I am sure it was Marty's potato pancakes that got her started. I ate them first at a Hanukkah celebration at their home.

2 medium yellow onions, peeled
4 medium baking potatoes, peeled
2 eggs
2 tablespoons matzoh meal
2 teaspoons kosher salt
  (or 1/2 teaspoon salt)
1/4 teaspoon black or white pepper
Vegetable oil for frying
Sour cream, lingonberries,
  cranberries, or applesauce
  for garnish

1. Grate the onions and potatoes with the fine mesh of a manual grater. Mix and pat down with paper towels to remove excess moisture.
2. In a large bowl, whisk the eggs. Add the onions, potatoes, matzoh meal, salt, and pepper.
3. Put a couple of tablespoons of oil in a large skillet or griddle and heat over medium-high heat until it is very hot (but not smoking!).
4. Drop two spoonfuls of potato mixture at a time into the skillet and flatten with a spatula. (You can probably fit 5 or 6 pancakes in the skillet at a time.) Cook about 4 minutes on each side until golden brown.
5. Remove to a platter lined with paper towels to drain. Cover with foil or put into a 200°F oven to keep warm.
6. Serve with a tablespoon of sour cream, applesauce, or both. Swedish lingonberries or cranberries are marvelous, too.
   Serves 4 to 6

The Mouse
and the Clock

Hickory, dickory, dock!

The mouse ran up the clock;

The clock struck one,

And down he run,

Hickory, dickory, dock!

The City Mouse and the Country Mouse

nce upon a time there lived two cousins, a city mouse and a country mouse.

One day, the city mouse received a letter from her country cousin, inviting her to come for a visit. Excited, she filled three suitcases with frilly hats, fancy outfits, and stylish shoes. Then she bought some bonbons for the train ride and set off for the country.

The city mouse arrived just as her country cousin was arranging some yellow wildflowers in a vase.

"Welcome!" the country mouse cried, giving her cousin a warm hug. She had just tidied up her small cottage, which sat at the foot of a shady tree alongside a babbling brook. "Let me show you around the country."

"After I unpack," the city mouse said, hoping her clothes weren't too wrinkled.

The City Mouse and the Country Mouse

The country mouse watched her cousin fill every closet and drawer in the house with clothes. Then she grabbed a basket for each of them and headed outside.

"Are we going shopping?" the city mouse asked, her eyes lighting up.

"Sort of," the country mouse said, heading toward a vegetable garden.

The city mouse watched her cousin fill her basket with tomatoes, beans, and corn. "This food grows in *dirt!*" she thought with disgust. But not wanting to seem ungrateful, she began filling her basket—after wiping everything off with a frilly handkerchief.

On their way home, the city mouse tripped on a root and her high-heeled shoe went flying into the brook.

"I'll get it!" her cousin cried, diving into the cool clear water. She grabbed the shoe and a small trout.

"Do you always work so hard for your dinner?" asked the city mouse, wiping off her shoe.

"I enjoy it," the country mouse said,

practicing her sidestroke. "Come take a dip."

"And get my clothes wet?" The city mouse raised an eyebrow.

The country mouse climbed out of the brook, wrung out her overalls, and said, "I'll prepare you a picnic you'll never forget."

The city mouse never did forget the meal the country mouse made for her—but not because she liked it. She found the fresh salad, broiled trout, and corn bread too simple and dull for her taste. Over a dessert of plain raspberries, she suggested the country mouse come to the city. "I'll show you a feast that you'll never forget."

So the next day, the country mouse, carrying a knapsack with a change of overalls, went to the city.

"Wow!" the country mouse said, amazed by the skyscrapers, the crowds, and the noise.

"Welcome to *my* home," said the city house, leading her cousin through a small door in a tall brownstone.

"I'm quite impress—" Suddenly a booming gong rang out. The country mouse plugged her ears and trembled with terror.

The City Mouse and the Country Mouse

"That's just the grandfather clock," the city mouse said with a laugh. Then she led her cousin into the dining room and up onto a long, shiny wood table.

"Yummm!" The country mouse drooled when she saw the platters of smoked salmon, pastries, and miniature sandwiches. It was teatime!

"Help yourself," the city mouse said, nibbling a caviar sandwich. The country mouse was about to bite into an éclair when— *Rrrrrrufff! Rrrrrrruff!* Two large dogs raced into the room.

"Hide!" the city mouse cried, diving under a china plate. The country mouse scampered into the folds of a napkin, quivering with fright.

When the dogs had gone, the country mouse grabbed her knapsack. "Good-bye, dear cousin," she said. "I'm going back to the country where I can eat in peace in my simple home."

"Good-bye, dear cousin," the city mouse said. "My life may be dangerous, but the fine dining and fancy clothes are worth it."

From that day on, the city mouse stayed in the city and the country mouse stayed in the country. And they sent each other postcards every month.

Animal

Why did the chicken
cross the road?
> To get to the
> other side.

Where do sheep
get haircuts?
> At a baa-baa shop.

What did the rooster's
ghost say every
morning at sunrise?
> Cock-a-doodle-boo!

Were do cows go
to see art?
> Moo-seums.

What do frogs order
at restaurants?
> Hamburgers and flies.

What do you say to a
bird on its birthday?
> Happy Bird-day!

What do birds say on
Halloween?
> *Trick or tweet!*

What has the head of a
dog, the tail of a dog,
but is not a dog?
> *A puppy.*

What keys are too big
to put in your pocket?
> *Donkeys, turkeys,*
> *and monkeys.*

If 1 pig, 2 cows,
5 chickens, 3 sheep,
and 1 big horse all
got under one tiny
umbrella, how many
animals would get wet?
> *None. It's not raining!*

If a rooster laid a white
egg and a brown egg,
what color chicks
would hatch?
> *None. Roosters don't*
> *lay eggs, hens do.*

Jokes

The Crocodile

Lewis Carroll

How doth the little crocodile
Improve his shining tail,
   And pour the waters of the Nile
   On every golden scale!

How cheerfully he seems to grin!
How neatly spread his claws,
   And welcomes little fishes in
   With gently smiling jaws!

Kite Tips

Go fly a kite! You have to do this at least once with your young child. There is something so great about a colorful kite soaring high above on a beautiful day. Will it reach the clouds? Chose a wide open space—young children tend to be enthralled for a while and then lose interest. They can at least run around while you stand there with the string, letting your mind soar for a bit longer.

1. Go buy a kite. Cheap and simple ones are readily available. It will fly better and everyone will be happier.

2. A simpler kite is better for novices. Delta-wings tend to be better choices than diamonds, boxes, or other more interesting designs because those can be unpredictable at first.

3. Sunny days with a gentle breeze are the best for flying kites.

4. Choose a place that's clear of trees and other obstructions. Good places are beaches or wide-open fields.

5. Begin by facing the wind and holding the kite up. As the wind starts to push against the kite, release a bit of line. Keep the line tight, releasing a little a a time, until the kite flies high.

6. If the kite begins to free-fall, you can regain control by moving in the direction of the plummet, taking in some line. If this doesn't help, try adding cord to the tail of the kite. If the kite keeps falling backwards, trim the tail.

7. Remember to let you child have a turn with the kite!

Dance to Your Daddy

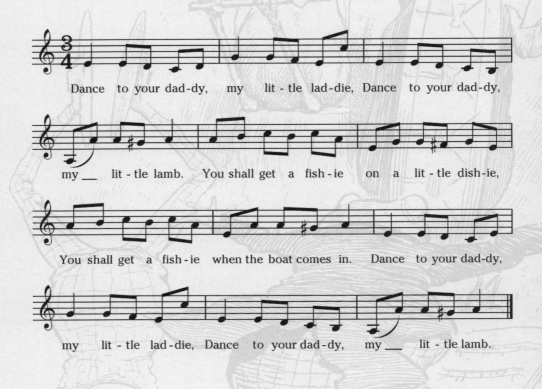

Dance to your dad-dy, my lit-tle lad-die, Dance to your dad-dy,

my __ lit-tle lamb. You shall get a fish-ie on a lit-tle dish-ie,

You shall get a fish-ie when the boat comes in. Dance to your dad-dy,

my lit-tle lad-die, Dance to your dad-dy, my __ lit-tle lamb.

THREE LITTLE DOLLIES

The Mistake Game

Rodger Kamenetz

I spoke to my daughter, Anya, in complete sentences when she was a conceptee and I listened for a response in her earliest cries. Some books recommended baby talk, and that was my wife, Moira's, language with Anya, but I preferred plain English. Why offer her ears a blurry target?

When it didn't drive me over the edge, her cry intrigued me. . . .

In her very first days, she learned to modulate her cries. Very quickly a parent learns the difference between the absolute pitch of "I'm in deep [trouble]" and the warble that simply declares discontent, or the more subtle mewling of "A little more milk would be just dandy." The baby is a practical philosopher: she knows her cry works. It speaks worlds—and moves them.

❖

Some parents can't get excited about a child's babble until the first words roll out. The competitive urge is enormous and in our culture we love anything we can count: "My child can say ten words." This stress on acquiring vocabulary overlooks a greater achievement: the melodies a baby can babble by the time she gets around to inserting *Dada* or *carcar* into a tune. Actually, the first words emerge singularly from the flow—like rocks jutting from a stream, around which melodies continue to swirl. A toddler's musical abilities outpace her vocabulary by far and this is as it should be.

Still, when Anya first spoke words, not sounds, I admit Moira and I were proud. Anya's first word uttered in Baton Rouge was recorded dutifully in her baby album. "Ball" seemed to

The Mistake Game

have universal application: my head was a ball, so was a head of lettuce in the A&P.

After "ball" came "No"; after "No," "Mama" and "Dada." I remember her sitting in the corner of the bedroom going, "Mama, Dada, Mama, Dada," looking left then right as if trying to place these important nouns properly in the universe.

By January, when she was sixteen months, she could say ball, bird, bottle, tee-tee (TV), bow-wow (dog), door, book, Mama, Ieeovu (I love you), car, bapu (apple), Dada, bath, bye-bye.

With this tiny vocabulary, Anya could already play what the philosopher Ludwig Wittgenstein calls a "language game."

"Ball," I said, and Anya motored off to her room, and returned with the ball. "Good," I said. "Car." She raced off and brought her toy car. "Anya," I said.

She puzzled for a minute, then laughed. I couldn't help myself: I had to tease her a little.

❖

Anya and I invented our own talking games as soon as Anya could talk. These were far more complex than Wittgenstein's "language games"—they were for pleasure only, and turned the world upside down. The most important one was the "mistake game."

"I woke up this morning and brushed my face, then I washed my teeth with soap. Was that a mistake?"

"Yes," she answered. "You should brush your teeth and wash your face with soap."

"Oh, I see. Then I put on my shoes and tied my socks. Was that a mistake?"

"Yes, Daddy. You should put on your socks and tie your shoes."

"I see."

The Mistake Game

I don't know how it started, exactly. The mistake game flew out of nowhere, a time filler at meals, a distraction while getting her dressed. The game mixed logic with the absurd, inflicting my sensibility on Anya. It also gave her a taste of role reversal, a chance, for once, to correct her illogical father.

It's wrong to tease children over-much. I've been guilty of it, going too far with the game, taking advantage of their sweet willingness to believe what an adult says.

A few times I drove Anya into screaming fits with my silly wordplay, forgetting she was still a child, in spite of her complex sentences and adult vocabulary. Other times, she'd laugh so hard we had to stop for fear of choking her.

"You're not Mommy, are you?" I'd say.
"No."
"I'm not Mommy either, am I?"

"Right." She'd nod her head sagely, knowing a new game was afoot.

"Well, if I'm 'not-Mommy,' and you're 'not-Mommy,' I must be you because we're both 'not-Mommy.'"

She'd splutter and laugh. "No, you're Daddy."

"I thought you said I was not-Mommy . . . "

Soon "not-Mommy" replaced the mistake game, hilarious to her and to me, too.

Teasing is a father's game of distance and closeness, a verbal shadowboxing or peekaboo. I'm here, I'm not here; I mean it, I don't. Whether the teasing heals or hurts probably depends on how secure the child is in that difficult quality, her father's love.

■

185

Puff the Magic Dragon

Words and Music by Peter Yarrow and Lenny Lipton

Puff the Mag - ic Dra - gon

lived by ____ the sea and

frol - icked in ____ the au - tumn mist ___ in a

land called Hon - a - lee. ____

Lit - tle Jack - ie Pa - per loved that ras - cal

Puff the Magic Dragon

Puff and brought him strings and seal - ing ___ wax and

(Chorus)

oth - er fan - cy stuff. Oh! Puff the Mag - ic

Dra - gon lived by ___ the sea and

frol - icked in ___ the au - tumn mist ___ in a

land called Hon - a - lee. _____

Puff the Mag - ic Dra - gon

Puff the Magic Dragon

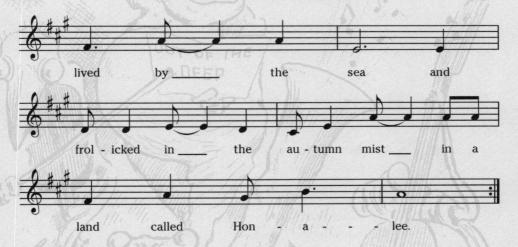

lived by _____ the sea and
frol - icked in ____ the au - tumn mist ___ in a
land called Hon - a - - - lee.

2. Together they would travel on a boat with billowed sail.
   Jackie kept a lookout perched on Puff's gigantic tail.
   Noble kings and princes would bow whene'er they came.
   Pirate ships would low'r their flag when Puff roared out his name. Oh! (Chorus)

3. A dragon lives forever, but not so little boys.
   Painted wings and giant rings make way for other toys.
   One gray night it happened, Jackie Paper came no more,
   And Puff that mighty dragon, he ceased his fearless roar.

4. His head was bent in sorrow, green tears fell like rain.
   Puff no longer went to play along the Cherry Lane.
   Without his lifelong friend, Puff could not be brave,
   So Puff that mighty dragon sadly slipped into his cave. Oh! (Chorus)

Beauty and the Beast

nce upon a time many years ago, there lived a rich ship merchant who had three sons and three daughters. His youngest daughter, Beauty, was the loveliest, which is how she got her name. Unlike her snooty sisters, Beauty loved to read, listen to music, and help around the mansion.

One night, the merchant's ships drifted away in a horrendous storm, making him a poor man. The following day, the family moved to a small, run-down farm.

"It's dirty here!" the oldest sister whined.

"It stinks!" the middle sister complained.

But Beauty was happy helping her father and brothers with the chores.

One day, the merchant heard that one of his ships had been found. Before setting off for the harbor, he asked his daughters what they wanted from town.

"A fancy dress," said the oldest sister.

"Silk hair ribbons," said the middle sister.

"A rose," said Beauty, "if you see one."

Beauty and the Beast

Their father's journey was a disaster; his ship sank before he arrived, and he got lost in the forest on his way home. As darkness fell, he saw a light in the distance and rode toward it. Soon, he found himself in front of a magnificent palace. Hungry and exhausted, he tied up his horse and knocked on the door. When no one answered, he walked right in.

Though the palace seemed deserted, supper was waiting on the table. He gobbled it up and fell asleep at the table. He awoke at sunrise, and found a hearty breakfast before him!

Before returning to his horse, the merchant plucked a rose for Beauty—and heard a frightful roar. A horrible beast was heading toward him.

"Ungrateful man!" the beast growled. "I gave you food and shelter, and you thank me by stealing a rose—my very favorite flower! For that I must kill you!"

"I, I only picked one rose, for my daughter Beauty," the merchant explained.

"Then I'll kill *her*," roared the beast, "if you can get her to come. If not, I'll kill you. Come back in three months!"

The merchant found his way home and told his children what had happened.

"We'll kill that awful beast," said his sons. But their father refused to let them go.

"It's all Beauty's fault," said the oldest sister.

"All for that stupid rose," said the middle sister.

For the first time, Beauty agreed with her sisters and insisted on returning to the beast's palace with her father three months later.

"Did your father make you come?" the beast roared as the three of them ate lunch.

"No," said Beauty. "It was my idea since I asked him to bring me the rose." She couldn't look the beast in the eye, for he was much too ugly.

After lunch, Beauty's father begged her to return home with him, but she stubbornly refused. So after a tearful good-bye, the merchant set off for the farm.

As she wandered around the beast's palace, Beauty felt sad and lonesome. Suddenly, she spied a sign on a door that said Beauty's Room. She opened the door and gasped, for it was the most beautiful room she'd ever seen. The wallpaper and bed-spread were patterned with roses, and the shelves were filled

with books she had never read.

"You're now the queen of the palace," the beast said, startling Beauty, for she hadn't seen him standing in the doorway. "Anything you wish for will be yours."

"I wish to see my poor father," Beauty said, stubbornly.

The beast handed her a magic mirror, which showed her father arriving home safely.

"Thank you," Beauty said, as the image melted away. She smiled for the first time all day.

"Would you mind if—" the beast began.

"What?" Beauty asked, surprised to see the beast's shy side.

"If I-I-I dine with you tonight," the beast finished.

"Not at all," said Beauty, grateful to have company.

When Beauty came down to supper, her favorite music was playing and her favorite meal was on the table.

"How did you know what I liked?" she asked the beast.

"I didn't," the beast said with surprise. "Mozart and macaroni and cheese are my favorites too."

After supper, the beast looked Beauty in the eye. "Do you think I'm terribly ugly?" he asked.

"Yes," Beauty said, unable to lie. "But I know you have a good heart."

"Then will you marry me?"

Beauty and the Beast

"*No!*" Beauty exclaimed in surprise, then wished she hadn't been so rude.

Over the next few months, Beauty began to enjoy living in the beast's palace. She read, listened to music, and wandered around the rose garden. The beast was kind and thoughtful, and seemed to forget his plan to kill her. (Not that Beauty ever reminded him!)

There were always roses in the dining room, and the beast joined Beauty for every meal. They talked about books and music and all their favorite things. The beast was such great company, Beauty soon got used to his ugliness.

But every night, when the beast asked her to marry him, Beauty refused. "I treasure our friendship," she said.

"Then promise you'll never leave me," said the beast.

"I promise," said Beauty, for she hadn't expected to return home anyway. But when the magic mirror showed her father sick in bed, she begged the beast to let her go see her father. "I'll be back in a week," she promised.

"I can't say no to you," said the beast, now deeply in love with Beauty. "But if you don't return, I'll die of misery." Then he slipped a magic ring on Beauty's finger. "You'll wake at home tomorrow morning," he explained. "When you're ready to return, lay this ring on your bedside table." And the next morning, Beauty was back at the farm.

"Beauty!" her father cried, jumping out of bed. Just seeing his youngest daughter alive cured him at once.

"Look at you! Where did you get such beautiful clothes?" asked the oldest sister.

"I thought you were going to be killed," said the middle sister.

Beauty just smiled secretly—for she now realized she was in love with the beast.

Despite her feelings, Beauty was needed at the farm, since her brothers had left for the army. So she stayed longer than a week.

One night, she dreamt that the beast was lying half-dead in the rose garden. Waking in tears, she laid the magic ring on the bedside table and fell asleep again. The next morning, she woke up in the beast's palace—but the beast was nowhere in sight.

She ran out to the rose garden and found the beast lying half-dead on the ground, just as he'd been in her dream. She filled a bucket with water and dumped it over his head.

The beast opened his eyes. "You forgot your promise, Beauty," he said weakly. "And now I'm dying. Love is so painful."

Beauty and the Beast

"But it's not!" Beauty cried. "Love is wonderful—and I know that because I love you and want you to be my husband."

Instantly, the palace blazed with light and music filled the air. And Beauty found herself looking into the eyes of a handsome prince.

"Where's the beast?" she asked looking around her.

"*I* was the beast," said the prince. "You see, a wicked fairy put a spell on me that only a beautiful maiden like you could break—and only if she fell in love with me despite my ugliness." He got up and led Beauty into the palace, where her father and her jealous sisters were waiting.

The following afternoon, Beauty and the prince were married, and they lived happily ever after—talking about books, listening to Mozart, eating macaroni and cheese, and smelling the roses.

My Brother Bert

by Ted Hughes

Pets are the hobby of my brother Bert.
He used to go to school with a mouse in his shirt.

His hobby it grew, as some hobbies will,
And grew and GREW and **GREW** until—

Oh don't breathe a word, pretend you haven't heard.
A simply appalling thing has occurred—

The very thought makes me iller and iller:
Bert's brought home a gigantic gorilla!

If you think that's really not such a scare,
What if it quarrels with his grizzly bear?

You still think you could keep your head?
What if the lion from under the bed

And the four ostriches that deposit
Their football eggs in his bedroom closet

And the aardvark out of his bottom drawer
All danced out and joined in the roar?

What if the pangolins were to caper
Out of their nests behind the wallpaper?

With the fifty sorts of bats
That hang on his hatstand like old hats,

And out of a shoebox the excitable platypus
Along with the ocelot or jungle-cattypus?

The wombat, the dingo, the gecko, the grampus—
How they would shake the house with their rumpus!

Not to forget the bandicoot
Who would certainly peer from his battered old boot.

Why it could be a dreadful day,
And what, oh what, would the neighbors say!

Animal Tracks

DOMESTIC CAT

Just after a fresh blanket of snow falls is the perfect time to look for animal tracks. Take your child outside and look for interesting indentations in the snow. Your child will marvel at these signs of "invisible visitors," and he or she will feel like real detectives when following the trails. Use the illustrations on these pages to help your child identify the animals that trek around your neighborhood in the wintertime. Go get that polar bear!

GREY SQUIRREL

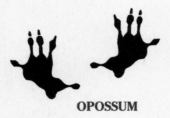

OPOSSUM

PORCUPINE

TURKEY

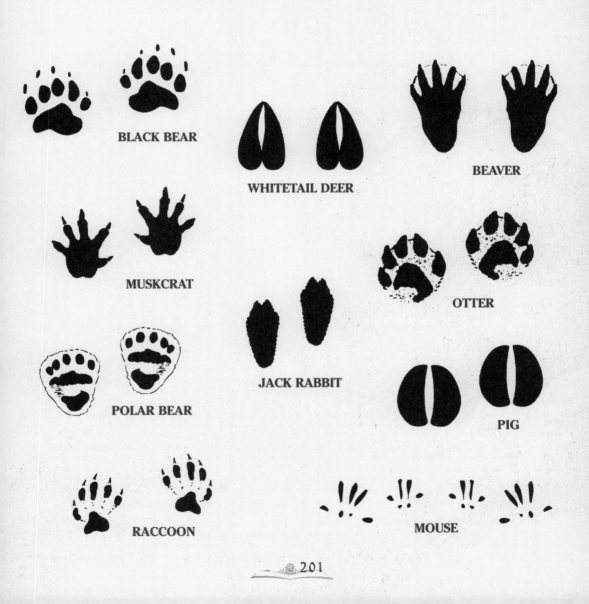

BLACK BEAR

WHITETAIL DEER

BEAVER

MUSKCRAT

OTTER

POLAR BEAR

JACK RABBIT

PIG

RACCOON

MOUSE

201

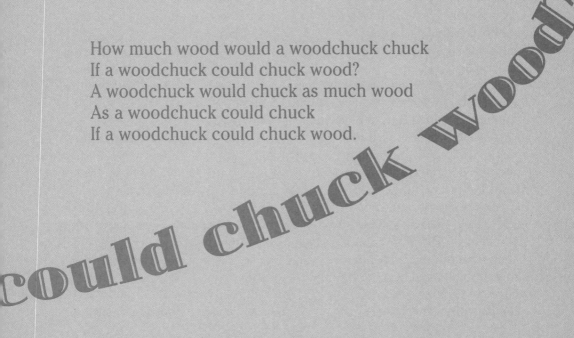

od would a
chuck
uck

How much wood would a woodchuck chuck
If a woodchuck could chuck wood?
A woodchuck would chuck as much wood
As a woodchuck could chuck
If a woodchuck could chuck wood.

could chuck wood?

For the Love of My Children

Kenny Loggins

Are we ever really free from the gravitational pull of the moon?

Can a child ever stop loving his father or needing his father's love? I don't think so. As I see it, this is simply "emotional physics."

I guess that's the good news and the bad news. We crave the love and acceptance of our fathers yet many of us may never truly obtain it this time around. Are we then destined to search for it in the eyes of lovers and friends the rest of our lives, like Diogenes in search of the honest man? And is this yearning just a hole no one else can ever really fill?

I now believe that somehow as I parent my children I begin to heal the wounds of my own childhood. Slowly, often painfully, I kneel in the dark, opening boxes of long-hidden memories and feelings I'd years ago assumed were better left unexamined, undisclosed even to myself, unchangeable and ultimately unnecessary.

There in the dark, but for the love of my children, they'd have stayed unearthed like so many dinosaur bones. "Who needs 'em?" I figured. "Who needs the pain?"

But the baby is born, and as those dinosaurs come screaming out into the light, trampling my well-placed life, trashing my carefully planted rows of plans, "You do!" is the only inevitable, loving and painful sound I hear within his birth-cry.

But I do have a choice . . . and yet I don't.

History wants to repeat itself, such is its vanity, so Crosby, my

For the Love of My Children

fourteen-year-old, plays guitar and writes his own songs. ("Hell, Dad doesn't work for a living, why should I?") He is my "outer face," and as such, presents himself to the world as the confident and street- wise performer I thought I wanted to be back then. Being fourteen he pulls me in and pushes me away all at the same time. He needs a male community to civilize him, but unfortunately in our world no such society seems to exist. So we dance alone.

To the south, in Los Angeles, my thirteen-year-old, Cody, now lives with his mother. Four or five days a month is barely enough to get to know him, or him me. This distance, physical and emotional, is the only great pain in my life. This constant longing is the kind people must simply shut-off to, or somehow learn to exist with, and is my biggest struggle.

Cody is my "inner face," and I know him as I know my secret heart. (Julia and I refer to him as "the heart with feet.") He is the "Karate-poet-comedian," stoic and intensely moral, and archetype of a kind of self-burning hero. Our time is yet to come. I know it will be tough, yet I long for it.

And lying next to me is baby Lukas Alushka. Almost two years old, he is a man on a mission. His name means Spirit Warrior, and sure, I know I've saddled him with my own lofty vision, but it is also my prayer for him.

Luke is the Lancelot to my Guinevere. He fire-walks with us, always reminding me to be joyful in the storm, "Life is bliss, isn't it?" He sighs. He is the third son of the third son of a third son. No legacy there, eh? No wonder I feel a sense of urgency to awake and walk consciously into my dream.

For the Love of My Children

For the love of my children I must again challenge the unknown, my hidden self. I will turn to face my own storm and make peace with my hurricane to keep from passing that storm on to my sons.

But I don't mean to say that my father was a bad guy who only screwed me up somehow. Please don't misunderstand me. He was a great guy. Gentle, loving and patient. He taught me how to play baseball, basketball (we were killers in our neighborhood at two-on-two), track (he was a champion hurdler in high-school), touch football, golf, as well as how to listen and make friends, how to notice the things others do, how to be a leader.

For the love of my father I became a performer and unknowingly fulfilled his unfulfilled dreams of the stage. But, dad passed on his demons too. I think a child believes that the act that truly proves and earns love is to become that parent. And so we take on all dad's emotional values and beliefs as well as his fast-ball and jump-shot. This becomes our heritage.

Yet, as I gain awareness of what's his and what's mine, I discover who's really here in this body. Slowly but surely I send this message of freedom to my own children: "I love you. You are free to be you, wherever that takes us."

Perhaps their father's ultimate legacy will be remembered as this:

You are never trapped.
You have the power to change your life . . . to make it better.
Setting yourself free is your greatest tribute to me.

For the love of my children, I can and will change.

Our Son
by Edgar A. Guest

He's supposed to be our son, our hope and our pride,
In him all the dreams of our future abide,
But whenever some act to his credit occurs
I never am mentioned, the glory is hers,
And whenever he's bad or has strayed from the line,
Then always she speaks of the rascal as mine.

When trouble has come she will soberly say:
"Do you know what your son has been up to today?
Your son spilled the ink on the living-room floor!
Your son broke the glass in the dining-room door!
I am telling you now something has to be done,
It is high time you started correcting your son!"

But when to the neighbors she boasts of his worth,
It is: "My son's the best little boy on the earth!"
Accuse him of mischief, she'll just floor you flat
With: "My son, I'm certain, would never do that!
Of course there are times when he's willfully bad
But then it's that temper he gets from his dad!"

Take Me Out to the Ball Game

Words by Jack Norworth   Music by Albert von Tilzer

Take me out to the ball - game.

Take me out with the crowd. _____

Buy me some pea - nuts and crack - er - jack.

I don't care if I nev - er get back. Let me

Take Me Out to the Ball Game

root,   root,   root   for   the   home   team.   If

they   don't   win   it's   a   shame. _____   For   it's

one,   two,   three   strikes,   you're   out   at   the

old   ball   -   game. _____

Tom, Tom,

Tom, Tom, the piper's son,

Stole a pig, and away he run

    The pig was eat,

    And Tom was beat,

And Tom ran crying down the street.

the Piper's Son

My Daughters

Rick Bass

It strikes me that a father's job is to provide constancy and stability—though I have met countless wonderful and admirable women who were raised by fathers and mothers who were anything but that. Nonetheless, it's what I believe—or what I want to believe. Certainly amid that desire to provide constancy is the notion of being not just a good father, but a good husband. I know or believe that constancy and repetitiveness can teach almost anything. I know to show by specific example, too, rather than by speaking in general abstractions. And again the problem seems to be not so much what to teach the girls. To encourage them,

for instance, to celebrate freedom and wildness is easy. But do I teach them to deal with stress, for example, as I do—by trying to avoid it? You want your daughters to loathe injustice, but do you want them to burn as erratically and out-of-control as you do—with that much bitterness?

And do I have any say in the matter anyway?

Constancy. I take pains to show them the constancy of the seasons up here—a kind of constancy-in-change, which my hunch tells me will be one of the most valuable lessons for the future: to appreciate constancy, yet adapt to change as it comes—to have a supple strength, rather than a rigid or brittle one.

My Daughters

Certain elements are bedrock in our lives: dried flowers hanging around the cabin, picked from each walk through the woods in summer; the gathering of berries, fish, meat, and mushrooms from the woods and streams; the gathering of each autumn's firewood. . . . I try to engage them in all of these cycles, and though it will be a long time before they can go hunting with me if they want to, they help me pluck and clean the birds I come home with. Right after Mary Katherine was born I had to take a teaching job for several weeks—all three of us went to Wisconsin—and I remember asking my young women students for tips and advice about being a father to daughters.

It amazed me how common their response was: that their fathers never spent quite enough time with them (the more beloved the father, the greater the desire was for more time); how their fathers never took them hunting or fishing enough. Only the boys got to go on those trips. The daughters I talked to had had a smattering of father-daughter camping trips, and then that was it, they turned eighteen, and were out of there.

It wasn't that the girls wanted so much to hunt or fish, it seemed, as they wanted to spend more time with their fathers watching their father be themselves.

It seems a simple thing to commit to; it seems like stating the obvious. But the commonality of my students' responses was so overwhelming that I resolved to do everything I could to keep my daughters from being

My Daughters

able one day to say such a thing. It chilled me to imagine my daughters being eighteen, nineteen, twenty years old, and saying to someone that they felt like they didn't get to spend enough time with me when they were growing up.

❖

I do not know how to staunch against the coming tides. I work at being more receptive to the joys of the moment—to inhaling them deeply. I try to be as constant as I can. I am firm and try, in the beautiful heat of my love, not to become manipulated. I try to stand firm.

Mary Katherine and Lowry and I are building a rock wall. It appears to have no rhyme or reason in the path it travels through the woods. We build it with certain rocks that we find along roadsides or in the woods—good squared-off sturdy rocks that won't get frost heaved in the transition between winter and spring each year, as the ground contracts and then swells, giving birth each year to new life.

The rock wall wanders—almost staggers, in places—through the woods, enclosing nothing, bounding and imprisoning nothing. We build it only because we like the beauty of it, and the durability of stone, and the way it fits the forest as it wanders up and down the hills, stable and secure, like a spine, or an earth anchor.

Both girls have their little work gloves. They trudge along behind me as I wrestle with some flat granite behemoth, sweat pouring off of

My Daughters

me. ("Sun-water," Mary Katherine calls it.) Sometimes we work deep into the evenings, beyond sunset. The stars begin to shine, and we keep working. "Look," Mary Katherine says, "the sky is all dressed up." Lowry points to the largest rocks, points to me, and says "Up," and then points to the wall.

We stack the rocks carefully. It feels good to be working with such heavy weight. The wall just keeps getting longer each year. It fits where it is. We lean against it and rest when we're tired. It's so strong—so stable. We could stare at it for hours. It's not going anywhere. It feels good to be building something real: a physical model, a representation, of the thing between us. It is like a map of our blood—of who and what we are to each other.

We work on it a little each day. It adds up, accumulating a mass that is dizzying to look at. It speaks not so much to who we are, as to who we would like to, or can, become. Every morning when I wake up and look out the window it lies there, within reach: a thing we have crafted together. The rock wall speaks to more than happiness. The rock wall is a leap of joy.

■

Rock Skipping

Rock skipping is a very cool "dad" skill. It can take a long time to perfect the throw that causes a rock to skip endlessly across a still lake or pond. Make sure you select a rock that is—above all—flat, relatively smooth, and somewhat round (otherwise you may sabotage your chances of that perfect skip). Follow the instructions below and maybe you'll be able to impress and pass on the technique. Otherwise, stick with rock collecting!

1. Find a still lake or pond and the "perfect" flat rock.
2. Skipping a rock across a lake isn't much different than tossing a Frisbee, except that you want it to skim the surface of the water rather than fly through the air. Hold the rock in your hand as you would a Frisbee, between your thumb and index finger, the rest of your fingers curled in your hand.
3. Toss the rock like a Frisbee, aiming straight across the surface of the water. Envision the rock skimming the surface of the water, rather than skipping (sometimes this helps).

FUN FACTS:
- Diamonds and emeralds are very rare and valuable rocks.
- Talc (soapstone) is the softest rock. Diamonds are the hardest rocks.
- The Egyptians built the pyramids five thousand years ago with limestone. They are still standing today.
- Rocks come in all different colors: black, white, gray, brown, pink, and yellow. See how many different rocks you can find!

Rock Collecting

Rocks are the oldest things your child can collect. Many of them are millions and millions of years old! Let your child start a collection of small rocks from different places he or she visits. Keep the rocks in shoeboxes or egg cartons, sorting them by color, texture, and shape. Teach your child about the different kinds of rocks:

> IGNEOUS rocks are formed when molten rock (often called lava) cools and hardens. These rocks are made up of tiny crystals that you can look for when identifying your rock. Granite and basalt are kinds of igneous rocks.
>
> SEDIMENTARY rocks are created by layers upon layers of minerals such as salt and sand, which settle and solidify into rocks. Often these rocks are recognizable by the different colors that you can see in them, which indicate the different layers. Sandstone, shale, and limestone are sedimentary rocks.
>
> METAMORPHIC rocks are igneous and sedimentary rocks that have been subjected to heat and pressure. They may be difficult to identify, but if the rock was originally sedimentary you might be able to see the different layers pressed very tightly together. Marble, soapstone, and slate are metamorphic rocks.

So long as enthusiasm
lasts, so long is youth
still with us.

—Anonymous

The Steadfast Tin Soldier

nce upon a time, in a large house on a tree-lined street, a boy tore the wrapping paper off a long wooden box— the last of his birthday presents.

"Tin soldiers!" he cried with delight, and those were the first words the twenty-five tin soldiers ever heard.

Each soldier, made from the tin of an old spoon, wore a splendid uniform with a tall helmet, carried a bayonet over his shoulder, and stared straight ahead. They all looked exactly alike–except for one.

"Grandma, why does this soldier have only one leg?" the boy asked.

"He was the last of the batch and I ran out of tin," said his grandmother.

But this "different" tin soldier stood just as firmly on one leg as the others stood on two. He liked being unique and admired the other unique toys on the table. His favorite was a large paper castle with a lake made from a small mirror.

"I wonder who lives there," he thought, and that's when he

noticed the graceful ballerina standing in the castle's doorway. She was made out of cardboard and wore a pretty muslin dress with a blue ribbon scarf to match. A tiny tinsel rose had been glued to the tip of the scarf.

The tin soldier admired the way the ballerina stretched her arms as she balanced herself on—gasp! He couldn't believe his eyes! For the ballerina also stood on only one leg! (He didn't realize that her other leg was raised so high it was hidden by her skirt.)

"She's lovely!" the tin soldier said to himself. "I must find a way to meet her so we may marry and. . . ." He suddenly had a disturbing thought. "She lives in a castle, so she must be a princess—and what would a princess want with a soldier who lives in a box with twenty-four roommates?"

"Clean-up time!" called a woman's voice.

The tin soldier quickly dove behind a closed-up jack-in-the box as the boy put away the other soldiers. From where he lay, he had a perfect view of the ballerina as she balanced daintily on one perfect leg.

That night, while the boy and his family were asleep, the toys came to life. They ran races, sang songs, told jokes, and turned cartwheels. What a noisy bunch! In fact, the only ones not making

The Steadfast Tin Soldier

any noise were the tin soldier and the ballerina.

Bang, bang, bang!

The tin soldier could hear the other soldiers trying to get out of their box. They wanted to join in the fun, but the lid was too heavy for them to lift.

Just as the clock struck midnight, the jack-in-the-box lid popped open and an ugly imp sprang out.

"Hey, tin soldier," the imp said in a raspy voice. "Keep your eyes to yourself! Otherwise you'll be sorry."

But the tin soldier was so intrigued by the ballerina, he kept right on staring. (He didn't know how evil imps could be.)

When the clock struck six, the toys scrambled back to their places and fell silent.

"Hello," said the boy's sister, picking up the tin soldier. She set him on the windowsill and went to eat breakfast.

In a sudden flash, the window flew open and the tin soldier felt a gust of wind push him down, down, down toward the street below. "The imp did this!" the tin soldier thought as he somersaulted toward the pavement.

Thump! He landed leg up, helmet down.

Thunder crashed, lightning lit the sky, and it began to rain and then pour.

The rain swept the tin soldier into the gutter. The water

carried the soldier through a dark, clammy drain down a dangerous waterfall and into a canal.

"Yikes!" the tin soldier wanted to yell. But that wouldn't have been proper. So he continued to look straight ahead as the water rose to his neck.

"I wish I could see the ballerina one last time," he thought, remembering how lovely she was.

GULP!

The tin soldier was swallowed by a big fish and everything went dark.

"It's darker than the box I used to share with the other tin soldiers!" the tin soldier thought. But, of course, he just looked straight ahead and remained silent.

After what seemed like several hours, the fish began to flip-flop violently. Then it became calmer—and finally stopped. A ray of light appeared.

"The tin soldier!" shouted a woman. "Isn't this the one that fell from the windowsill?" You see, the fish had been caught and sold in the fish market to the cook who worked in the boy's home. When the cook came home, she brought the fish to the kitchen, cut it open—and out popped the tin soldier.

"It's him!" cried the boy. He grabbed the tin soldier, brought him to the table of toys, and lined him up with the other soldiers.

The Steadfast Tin Soldier

From the corner of his eye, the tin soldier could see the large paper castle, the lake, and the ballerina—who looked as beautiful as ever on her one leg. He felt so much love for her, he nearly cried—but that wouldn't have been soldierlike.

"Gotcha!" yelled the boy's sister. She grabbed the tin soldier and threw him into the fire.

"This is the imp's doing!" the tin soldier thought angrily, as his colors began to fade. But he remained steadfast and silent as the hot flames surrounded him. As he began to melt, he took one last look at the ballerina—and, to his amazement, she was looking right back at him!

Suddenly, a gust of wind blew the cardboard ballerina into the fire. She blazed up instantly and was gone.

The next morning, among the ashes lay a heart-shaped lump of tin. And on that heart was the tinsel rose—now black as coal—that had been glued to the ballerina's scarf. The little boy picked up the tin heart and the tinsel rose, put them together in a little box, and put the box to the very top of his bookshelf.

As time went on, the boy grew up and forgot about his toys and the little box on his shelf. And so the tin heart and the tinsel rose stayed there together forever and ever.

Going Fishing

A goldfish is a wonderful first pet to test the waters with. If your child shows continued interest, you can graduate to a larger tank and more fish. And before that first real fishing trip, let you child try some indoor fishing. By creating your own stock of fish, you can be sure the catch will be plentiful!

A FISH OF YOUR OWN
goldfish, fish bowl, water pump filter, food

1. Purchase a nice, vibrant Betta (Siamese fighting fish) and good sized bowl from your local pet store. It is also a good idea to get a small pump filter to help keep the water clear and to aerate the water.
2. Don't release the fish from the bag of water into the tank right away. Float the bag in the water for about half an hour until the temperature equalizes. This lets the fish adjust to the change.
3. Now for the fun part. Keeping goldfish is pretty easy, so you can teach your child how to take care of the fish. Feed it once or twice a day, depending on what the pet store says, and make sure not to overfeed. Fish always have the appearance of looking hungry, and they will notoriously stuff themselves to death if you let them.

INDOOR FISHING
stick or small broom handle, string, large paper clip, construction paper

1. To make the fishing pole, use the stick or small broom handle, tying string to one end.
2. For a hook, uncoil the paper clip and tie it to the end of the string.
3. For fish, cut 1 x 3-inch strips of different colored construction paper.
4. Fold the paper in half making a V shape.
5. Scatter the Vs on floor, upside down, so that your child can hook them onto the paper clip.

Fish

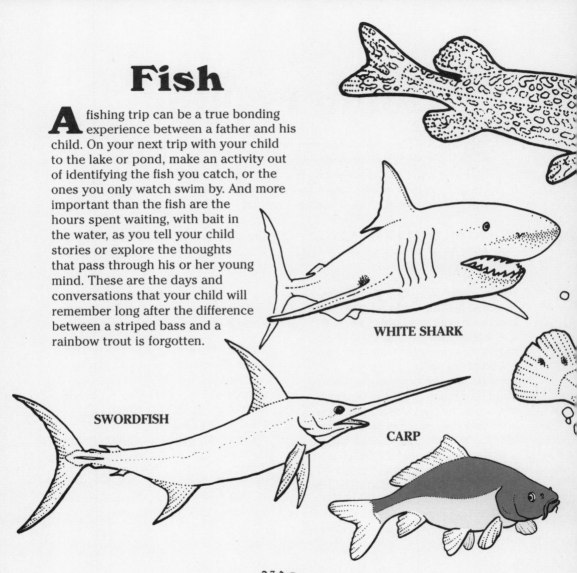

A fishing trip can be a true bonding experience between a father and his child. On your next trip with your child to the lake or pond, make an activity out of identifying the fish you catch, or the ones you only watch swim by. And more important than the fish are the hours spent waiting, with bait in the water, as you tell your child stories or explore the thoughts that pass through his or her young mind. These are the days and conversations that your child will remember long after the difference between a striped bass and a rainbow trout is forgotten.

WHITE SHARK

SWORDFISH

CARP

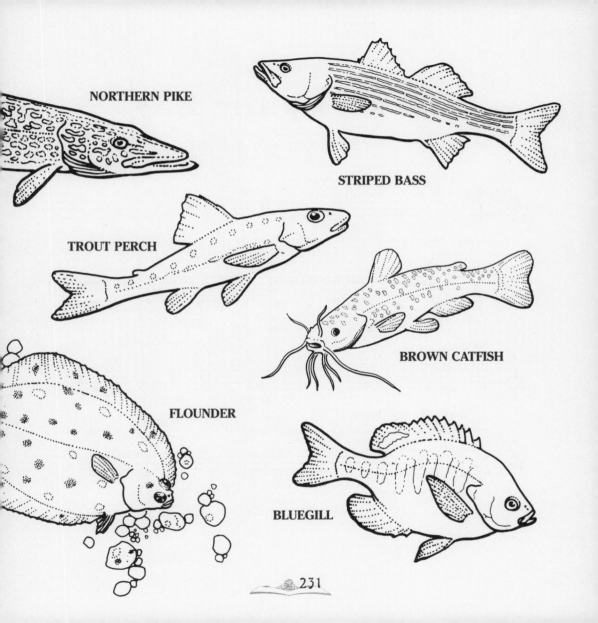

NORTHERN PIKE

STRIPED BASS

TROUT PERCH

BROWN CATFISH

FLOUNDER

BLUEGILL

Down by the Bay

Down   by   the   bay,   echo: Down   by   the

_ where the wa - ter - mel - ons grow,
bay, where the wa - ter - mel - ons

_ Back to my home, ____ I dare not go,
grow, Back to my home, I dare not

_ For if I do,
go, For if I

232

Down by the Bay

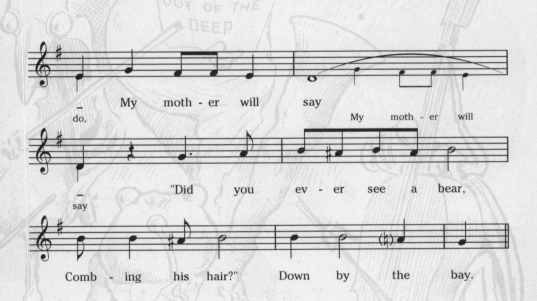

My moth - er will say

do,

My moth - er will

"Did you ev - er see a bear,

say

Comb - ing his hair?" Down by the bay.

2. "Did you ever see a bee
   With a sunburned knee?"

3. "Did you ever see a moose
   Kissing a goose?"

4. "Did you ever see a whale
   With a polka-dot tail?"

(Continue by making up own verses)

A Day at the Beach

For many children, that first trip to the seashore is the official sign that summer has indeed begun. With crowds of people, a gently crashing surf, and an endless array of exotic things to see and touch, the beach may be one of the most interesting places you can take your child. He or she will be entranced by all the new sights and sounds, but it may also be possible for you to suggest a few activities.

DIGGING FOR TREASURES

Toddlers may be a little intimidated by the sounds and vastness of the ocean on their first visit of the summer. Focus their attention on a little patch of sand. Bury a few of their favorite little toys (figurines or cars) in a circle around them. (For younger children, let the toys stick up a bit out of the sand to make them easier to find.) Provide shovels and let them dig for their treasures.

DIGGING FOR SAND CRABS

Near the water's edge, dig into the sand to about the depth of your hand. You should be able to see sand crabs scurrying about, burrowing under the sand.

SAND ANGELS

Just like snow angels, but in the sand.

BURYING DAD

A favorite. Dig a shallow area to lay in, get comfortable, and let your kids cover you with sand.

WRITING ON SAND

Find a stick on the beach and try scratching giant letters and shapes, tic-tac-toe, and hopscotch in the sand.

FINDING THE BEST SEASHELLS

If you have time, go walking along the beach at low tide and note where the most debris is—these will be the places where the most shells will be collected at high tide. Return to these spots in the morning just after high tide and pick through to find the shells you want to keep.

Sandcastles

No trip to the beach is complete without a sandcastle, or at least a really good attempt at making one. Take along buckets, pails, small hand shovels, and anything that will serve as a mold. Younger children are happy with the simplest of shapes to stomp on. Try building a series of mounds—like an obstacle course for them to weave through without knocking over the shapes. For older children, impress them with these sand structure techniques.

DRIBBLY SAND

1. Select a spot not so close to the shoreline that the waves will reach you, but not too far away, either. Dig a hole until the sand has a very watery consistency.
2. Build a small mound of sand that you can dribble onto.
3. Scoop up a bit of wet sand from the hole. Shape your hand into a fist, hold it a few inches above the mound, and allow sand to "leak" from the bottom of your fist. The wet sand should stick and form dribbly shapes along the sides of the mound.

TOWER BUILDING

1. Squeeze handfuls of wet sand into a pancake shapes, by patting your hands around and using slight pressure. Don't press too hard or the water will be squished out the sides.
2. Stack the cakes on top of one another. As you near the top, begin to use smaller cakes so that the tower will taper off. This will allow for more stability as you and your child carve a fanciful tower with your own decorations.

WALL BUILDING

1. This is good for attaching towers, making stairs, or for creating anything else your imagination compels you to. Using cupped hands, scoop up some wet sand. Hold the sides of the scooped sand between your flattened palms and shake them so that the sand takes a brick-ish shape.
2. Lay the bricks from end to end until you reach your desire length, then begin stacking one on top of the other (a good, fun practice at masonry).

from The Bed Book

by Sylvia Plath

Most Beds are Beds
For sleeping or resting,
But the *best* Beds are much
More interesting!

Not just a white little
Tucked-in-tight little
Nighty-nighty little
Turn-out-the-light little
    Bed—

    Instead
A Bed for Fishing,
A Bed for Cats,
A Bed for a Troupe of
    Acrobats.

The *right* sort of Bed
(If you see what I mean)
Is a Bed that might
Be a Submarine

Nosing through water
Clear and green,
Silver and glittery
As a sardine.

Or a Jet-Propelled Bed
For visiting Mars
With mosquito nets
For the shooting stars . . .

Sailing Sailing

Sail - ing, sail - ing, o - ver the bound - ing main; _____ For man - y a storm - y wind shall blow ere Jack comes home a - gain. _____ man - y a storm - y wind shall blow ere Jack comes home a - gain. _____

Knots

Knots are an ancient tool and among humankind's oldest inventions. There are all different kinds of knots for many different purposes. It will be interesting for your child to learn about other kinds of knots when learning to tie a shoelace. Meanwhile, try using the bowline knot to create a little leash for your child's stuffed dog or the fisherman's bend to create a pull for a cardboard box wagon.

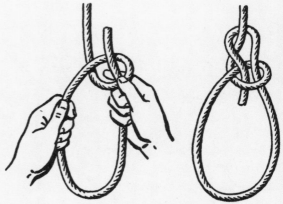

A **BOWLINE KNOT** is used to tie a loop in a rope end.

A **FIGURE EIGHT** is the most commonly used stopper knot to prevent a rope from passing through an opening.

A **BEND** is a type of knot used to unite two rope ends together to lengthen a rope. The **SHEET BEND** is a general utility bend that is easily remembered and can be tied in an instant.

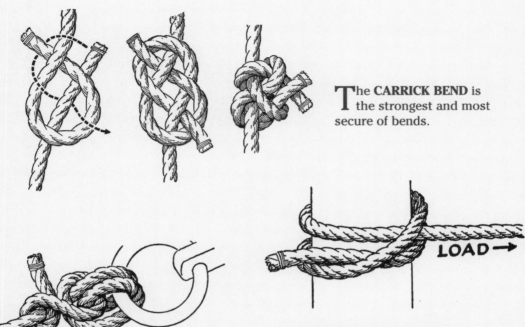

The **CARRICK BEND** is the strongest and most secure of bends.

The **FISHERMAN'S BEND** is one of the strongest of all hitches. It is often used to bend (tie) a rope to an anchor—hence the reason for this hitch being termed a bend.

LOAD →

A **HITCH** is a type of knot used to make a rope fast to various objects. The Clove Hitch is the quickest hitch to tie and easiest to remember but is not very secure. It is the most common hitch used in dock lines as a temporary mooring.

She sells seashells on the seashore;
The shells that she sells are seashells I'm sure.
So if she sells seashells on the seashore,
I'm sure that the shells are seashore shells.

Seashore

Legend has it that if you break the center of a sand dollar, five doves will be released from Heaven to spread goodwill and peace, making it one of the most valuable treasures to be found at the seashore. But there are many other things to be gained there as well. From shells to crustaceans to birds, a trip to the beach can be an educational and memorable experience, as your child learns about the different animals that live in and near the sea. On these pages are some common sights that you and your child can look for on your next visit to the beach—and don't forget to take home a few shells to remember your outing by!

SEAGULL

SEA URCHIN

GHOSTCRAB

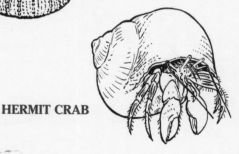

HERMIT CRAB

248

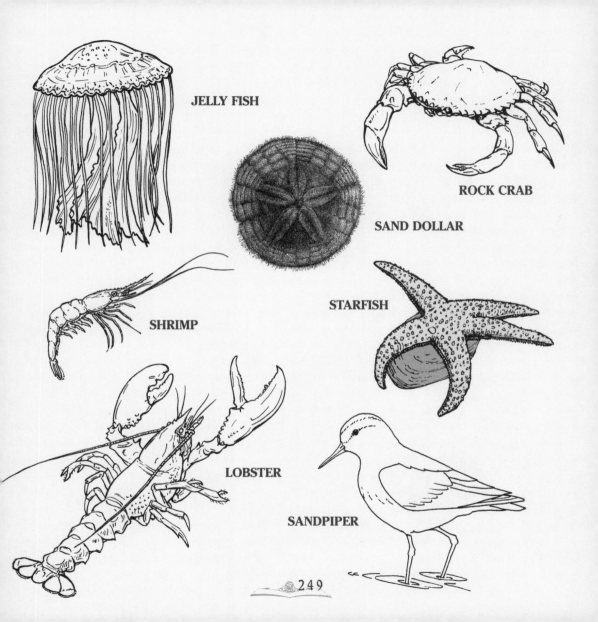

JELLY FISH

ROCK CRAB

SAND DOLLAR

SHRIMP

STARFISH

LOBSTER

SANDPIPER

249

To unpathed waters,

undreamed shores.

—William Shakespeare

A Prayer for Connection

Samuel Shem

"Let's go on our adventure, daddy."

This, our ritual at our beach in the summer, is to take the most difficult way from our beach towel to the lighthouse. Even when the tide is low and we could walk on the sand, Katie insists that we climb the rocks together to get there. She leads. I cheer her spirit as I follow her, she lithe and daring, I creaky and wondering which little piece of my musculoskeletal system will betray me first, compiling a list not only of what hurts at present but of just how far along the healing process are my injuries from the near and more distant past. What about that ankle sprain from stepping in a hole running for a cab in Boston at night last April? What about the old lateral meniscus tear from my first running experiences in the Dordogne in 1975? She pops along ahead; I follow, full of admiration.

We have tried to share with her, our Zen master, whatever awareness we have of the realm of the spirit—which we don't understand, of course, but which we conceive of as something else, some power greater than ourselves. For instance, every night at dinner we join hands and close eyes and she says, "Peace." We squeeze hands and eat. But we haven't really spoken about prayer. And so one day at the lighthouse, overlooking the expanse of sea and sky, I suggest to Katie that she and I offer a prayer. I start to explain what a prayer is. She interrupts:

"Daddy, I *know*. We pray to the Goddess."

A Prayer for Connection

"The 'goddess'?"

"Yeah. Momma told me all about her." She sighs, and says, resignedly, "Ohh-kay."

With mixed delight I realize that Janet has gotten there slightly ahead of me. Katie leads the prayer:

"To the Goddess who made everything and all the animals."

"Amen," I say.

❖

Katie, we pray to be with you in whatever sorrow. Pray that we will not be incapacitated at the time. And that together we will tilt your sorrow to compassion and understanding.

We hope for your connections with all the goddesses and the gods, for they are forever and ever and will help you when we are gone.

May our connection continue to grow, us two, us three—and your connection with a community of like-minded others.

And I pray that you will hold the spirit of connection so tightly and lightly that when the forces of disconnection wash over you with all the killing power of acid rain from Ohio or all the unnatural busy destructive garbage of TV and the Internet, you will be aware of its solidity, for that spirit of mutual connection is the only comfort in the whole world.

And I pray that when the hormones flow like sap you don't twist yourself out of your authentic self for the sake of anyone, boy or girl, and that you never mutilate yourself for anyone else or with tattoos

A Prayer for Connection

and body piercings. I pray for your relational integrity which can't help but assure your marvelous self, just as our love assures your growth.

And—because so far, you may recall, your total intake of vegetables has been seven sprigs of broccoli in five and three-quarter years—I pray you learn to eat green leafy vegetables.

And I pray for your spiritedness that makes you act like you already know everything, like when you were not yet three and you were talking on and on about something and I said to you, "Katie, you're perseverating," and you said, "Yeah, daddy, I know."

And I pray for your laughter, for one thing I have come to understand in my life of fifty-three years is that divinity resides in shared laughter, especially the guileless laughter of a child; so that once, when you were about two and a half and we were in a cab coming home from an airport and I asked you if your nose was running and you said, "No, it's walking!" in that screech of joy from you and the clatters of laughter from me and Momma and the African-American cabby were all the goddesses and gods a person could ever want, and they were laughing, too.

◼

Row, Row, Row Your Boat

Row, row, row your boat

gent - ly down the stream;

Mer - ri - ly, mer - ri - ly, mer - ri - ly, mer - ri - ly,

life is but a dream.

Toy Boats

There are lots of ways to make toy boats and rafts: half a walnut shell can be a sailboat with just a tiny piece of clay in the hull, and a toothpick for a mast. Here are instructions to make a twig raft and a fun and speedy craft capable of maneuvering down any river of imagination or fantasy:

TWIG RAFT
popsicle sticks, glue, a twig, colored paper

1. Glue the popsicle sticks side by side to create the base of the raft. Keep adding sticks until you reach your desired width.
2. Glue two sticks across the width of the raft perpendicular to the base; Place them toward the middle, keeping a space between them just wide enough to later support the twig mast.
3. When the glue is dried, turn the raft over and glue two sticks into place across the width again, near each end of the raft.
4. Let dry, turn over, and secure the twig mast in place, using a dollop of glue to hold. When dry, glue on a sail made from the colored paper.
5. Allow the glue to dry. When all is ship-shape, your child will be ready to set sail on a wild adventure in the bathtub.

SPEEDBOAT
scissors, milk carton, balloon

1. Using the scissors, cut the milk carton in half lengthwise. This should produce a boat-like shape.
2. Taking one of the halves, cut a round hole about half an inch in diameter in the middle of the flat bottom end.
3. Push the neck of the balloon through the hole, starting from the inside of the boat. Inflate the balloon, keeping the neck pinched close, and place the boat in the water. Releasing the neck will propel the boat through the water.

Trees

Trees are one of the oldest living things on Earth. They are also the largest (even older and larger than the dinosaurs!). Whether they have a treehouse, can't wait to decorate the Christmas tree, or simply love the taste of maple syrup, children are a tree's most natural friends. Taking your child on a nature walk to identify different types of trees is a great way to introduce him or her to Mother Nature. Use these illustrations to identify the trees where you live, and to teach your child the names of his or her leafy friends.

HEMLOCK

FLOWERING DOGWOOD

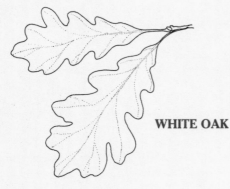

WHITE OAK

BALSAM FIR

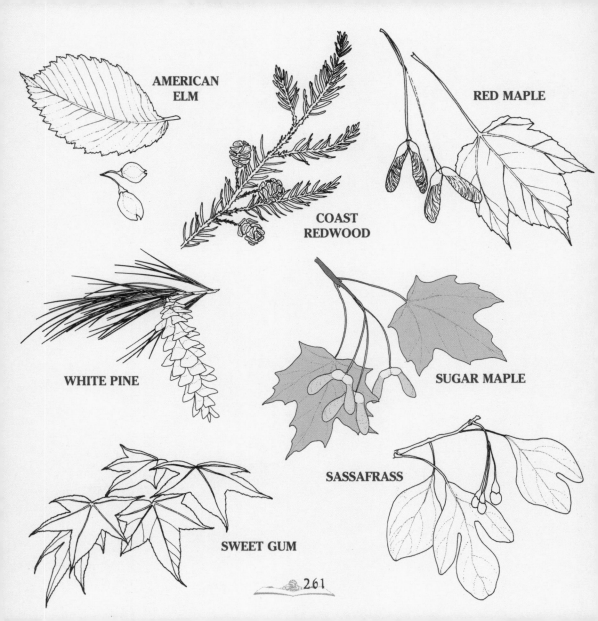

AMERICAN ELM

COAST REDWOOD

RED MAPLE

WHITE PINE

SUGAR MAPLE

SASSAFRASS

SWEET GUM

261

Swan swam over
Swim, swan
Swan swam
Well swum

Daddy Fell into the Pond

by Alfred Noyes

Everyone grumbled. The sky was grey.
We had nothing to do and nothing to say.
We were nearing the end of a dismal day,
And there seemed to be nothing beyond,
   THEN
Daddy fell into the pond!

And Everyone's face grew merry and bright,
And Timothy danced for sheer delight.
"Give me the camera, quick, oh quick!
He's crawling out of the duckweed."
Click!

Then the gardener suddenly slapped his knee,
And doubled up, shaking silently,
And the ducks all quacked as if they were daft
And it sounded as if the old drake laughed.

O, there wasn't a thing that didn't respond
  WHEN
Daddy fell into the pond!

Every survival kit
should include a
sense of humor.
—Anonymous

Three Wise Men

Three wise men of Gotham

Went to sea in a bowl;

If the bowl had been stronger,

My song had been longer.

of Gotham

The Boy Who Cried Wolf

Once upon a time, a shepherd boy lived in a tiny village high in the tallest mountains. Every morning, he led the villagers' sheep up a steep, grassy hill to graze.

From the shady spot where he sat, he'd often look down at the ant-size villagers and wondered what it would be like to bake bread, give haircuts, or cobble shoes for a living, surrounded by other people instead of sheep. "It wouldn't be as boring as watching sheep," he muttered. "All sheep do is eat and sleep and say *Baa* all day. I'm so, sooooo bored!" Suddenly, he had idea.

"Wolf! Wolf!" he cried loudly. "A wolf is chasing the sheep!"

The villagers immediately dropped what they were doing and hurried up the hill.

"I don't see a wolf," said the butcher, huffing and puffing from the steep climb.

"Our sheep are fine. What is going on here?" said the doctor, wiping the sweat from his brow.

"Oh! I just wanted some company!" said the shepherd boy.

"Don't cry 'wolf' when there's no wolf, or you'll be sorry," the

villagers scolded the shepherd boy. But the boy was laughing so hard tears ran down his cheeks.

The next day, from the shady spot where he sat, he looked down at the ant-size villagers again. And again he said, "All sheep do is eat and sleep and say *Baa* all day. I'm so, sooooo bored!" So again the boy yelled, "Wolf! Wolf! A wolf is chasing the sheep!"

Again, the villagers climbed the steep hill.

"I don't see a wolf," said the butcher, huffing and puffing even more than the day before.

"He did it again!" yelled the doctor.

"DON'T CRY 'WOLF' WHEN THERE IS NO WOLF, OR YOU'LL BE SORRY," they warned. But the shepherd boy just laughed, thrilled that he'd made his life more fun.

The next day it happened. From the top of the hill the boy saw a REAL wolf—furry, fierce, and drooling—sneaking from tree to tree, closer and closer.

"Wolf! Wolf!" the shepherd boy shouted in a panic. "WOLF! WOLF!"

The villagers heard him. But the butcher said, "He's doing it again!" And the doctor said, "I'm not running up that hill for nothing again." They thought the shepherd boy was trying to fool them like the two days before. This time they didn't come. And, just as the villagers had warned, the shepherd boy sure was sorry. With no one to help him, the shepherd boy lost all his sheep to the wolf.

The Boy Who Cried Wolf

Oh, the Places You'll Go!
by Dr. Seuss (Theodore Driesel)

Congratulations!
Today is your day.
You're off to Great Places!
You're off and away!

You have brains in your head.
You have feet in your shoes.
You can steer yourself
any direction you choose.
You're on your own. And you know what you know.
And *YOU* are the guy who'll decide where to go.

You'll look up and down streets. Look 'em over with care.
About some you will say, "I don't choose to go there."
With your head full of brains and your shoes full of feet,
you're too smart to go down any not-so-good street.

And you may not find any
you'll want to go down.
In that case, of course,
you'll head straight out of town.

It's opener there
in the wide open air.

Out there things can happen
and frequently do
to people as brainy
and footsy as you.

And when things start to happen,
don't worry. Don't stew.
Just go right along.
You'll start happening too.

OH! THE PLACES YOU'LL GO!

Jack

Jack be nimble,

Jack be quick,

Jack jump over
the candle-stick.

I've Been Working on the Railroad

I've been work-ing on the rail - road all the live - long day.

I've been work-ing on the rail - road just to pass the time a - way.

Don't you hear the whis-tle blow - ing, rise up so ear - ly in the morn?

Don't you hear the cap-tain shout - ing, "Di - nah, blow your horn!"

I've Been Working on the Railroad

Di - nah won't you blow, Di - nah won't you blow,

Di - nah won't you blow your horn, your horn"

Di - nah won't you blow, Di - nah won't you blow,

Di - nah won't you blow your horn?

Some - one's in the kitch - en with Di - nah,

I've Been Working on the Railroad

Some - one's in the kitch - en, I know, I know.

Some - one's in the kitch - en with Di - nah,

Strum - min' on the old ban - jo. Sing - ing

Fee, fie, fid-dle-e - i - o. Fee, fie, fid-dle-e - i - o - i - o.

Fee, fie, fid-dle-e - i - o, Strum - min'on the old ban - jo.

Aladdin and the Magic Lamp

nce upon a time, a poor tailor lived in a rich city in China. When he died, he left a wife, who had to spin cotton to earn a living, and a son named Aladdin.

One day, a strange man approached Aladdin in the street, pretending to be his uncle.

"I don't have an uncle," Aladdin said to the man, who was really an evil magician.

The magician insisted, and asked Aladdin to go for a walk with him. "If you come with me, I will make you a rich man," he said.

"Well, I'm not allowed to talk to strangers," said Aladdin. "But I'm sure my mother won't mind if I come home rich." And so they set off through the city, across fancy gardens and shady parks, and into the open country.

When they reached a narrow valley the magician said, "Mimbo! Limbo!" and *boom!* The earth cracked open before them.

"Wow!" Aladdin exclaimed, as he stared down into darkness.

"There's a door down there," the magician said. "I'm too big to fit through it, but you're not. Do as I say, and you'll be richer than

Aladdin and the Magic Lamp

the richest king."

"I will," Aladdin said, listening closely.

"Jump down," the magician instructed. "Then go through the door and walk until you reach a shelf. Take the lamp off the shelf and bring it to me. And don't touch anything besides the door and the lamp—or you'll die instantly!"

Then the magician took a ring from his pinkie finger and slid it onto Aladdin's middle finger. "This will protect you against evil."

Aladdin jumped into the hole and landed in soft dirt. He opened the door and hurried toward the shelf with the lamp. He stuffed it into a pocket and began to head back when something sparkly caught his eye.

He looked around and realized he was in an orchard. Fruits of the richest colors—red as rubies, green as emeralds, blue as sapphires—hung from the trees. Some were even as clear as diamonds! Forgetting his promise, Aladdin filled his pockets with the fruit, which he thought was made of glass, before returning to the magician, who peered down impatiently.

"Give me the lamp," the magician said.

Aladdin reached into his pockets, but there was so much fruit, he couldn't get to the lamp.

"Help me out first!" Aladdin said, extending his hand.

But the magician had no intention of letting Aladdin out at all.

Aladdin and the Magic Lamp

He just wanted the lamp. When Aladdin didn't obey him, he went into a rage. "Limbo! Mimbo!" he shouted, and *boom!* The earth slammed shut, leaving the boy alone in the darkness. Aladdin cried, "Help!" but his echo was the only answer. Very frightened, he began to cry, and rubbed his face to wipe away the tears.

"I AM THE SLAVE OF THE RING! WHAT IS YOUR WISH?" sounded a voice in the darkness.

Aladdin realized he'd accidentally rubbed the ring, his protection against evil.

"I want to be back home!" Aladdin said. And instantly, he was.

When he told his mother what had happened, she scolded him for going off with a stranger. "The fruit *is* pretty," she added, "but why would anyone want this dusty old lamp?" She began to rub off the dirt—and a genie appeared!

"WHAT IS YOUR WISH?" asked the genie, wiping dust from its eyes.

Too frightened to speak, Aladdin's mother handed the lamp to her son.

"Fetch us a feast," Aladdin said, for he was hungry and all they had in the cupboard were three stale rolls. Instantly the table was covered with silver platters of only the finest food and two silver cups filled with the sweetest tea in the world.

"Yummy!" Aladdin exclaimed, munching on a leg of lamb.

Aladdin and the Magic Lamp

"Chocolate truffles!" exclaimed his mother, popping one into her mouth.

They ate and ate until nothing was left. And the next morning, they sold the silver platters and cups for forty piles of gold, making them very rich.

One day, a few years later, the sultan (which means "king") announced that everyone should stay out of the streets while his daughter walked to her bath. But Aladdin, now a young man, ignored him. Instead, he hid in a doorway and glimpsed the princess as she passed with her maids. He was stunned by her beauty.

"I'm in love with the princess," Aladdin later told his mother. "I shall marry her!"

"Are you crazy?" said his mother. "We may be rich, but we are not royalty."

"I want you to go impress the sultan for me," Aladdin said confidently.

"Me!" cried his mother, though she knew it would be the proper thing to do. "But I have no valuable gift to present to him."

"The colorful fruit," Aladdin suggested.

"But they're only made of glass!" Aladdin's mother said.

"No," said Aladdin, who had taken them to a gem expert. "They are actually precious gems, and very valuable."

Aladdin and the Magic Lamp

So Aladdin's mother folded the fruit into fine cloth and set out for the palace.

"How exquisite!" the sultan cried when he saw the gems. "Even I have never seen such riches."

But although Aladdin's mother won the sultan's favor, he had already promised his daughter to an officer. "Here's what you must do," he said, admiring an emerald pear. "Have your son send me forty golden barrels of these gems delivered by forty costumed slaves, and he can marry my daughter." Aladdin's mother bowed and left, thinking all was lost.

When his mother broke the news to him, Aladdin immediately called the genie and repeated the sultan's request. The following day, a procession of forty costumed slaves marched through town, each carrying a golden barrel of diamonds, emeralds, rubies, and sapphires on his head. People watched with awe—but no one was more astonished than the sultan. "A wedding shall be planned at once," he pronounced.

Aladdin's mother, who had followed behind the slaves, was so excited she skipped all the way home. Aladdin, too, was overjoyed. He called the genie and wished for

Aladdin and the Magic Lamp

a marble palace fit for himself and the princess—and his mother. He also asked for a white horse and forty thousand pieces of gold. As he rode to the palace, he tossed gold into the streets, winning the affection of the people. And when the princess met Aladdin, she fell in love at once and the couple lived happily for years.

Then one day, the magician, who never dreamt Aladdin could have escaped from the cave, looked into his crystal ball and saw Aladdin rich and happy. He left his home in Africa and set off for China in a rage.

When he reached the palace, he was told Aladdin was out hunting.

"Then I must work fast," he said to himself, whipping up five shiny copper lamps. "Trade old lamps for new lamps!" he cried, setting up shop beneath the princess's window.

Hearing the magician's cry, the princess grabbed Aladdin's old lamp—not knowing about the genie—and hurried outside. "Here," she said, thinking the stranger must be stupid to take an old lamp for a new one.

The magician gave the princess a new lamp, hurried into the

Aladdin and the Magic Lamp

forest, and rubbed the old one. When the genie appeared, the magician ordered him to take Aladdin's palace and the princess to Africa. Immediately, the palace and the princess disappeared magically.

Deeply grieved by the disappearance of his daughter, the sultan sent for Aladdin. "If you don't find my daughter in forty days, I'll chop off your head," he told his son-in-law.

Feeling more sad than afraid, Aladdin searched all over China for his wife and palace but had no luck. Frustrated, he put his head in his hands.

"I AM THE SLAVE OF THE RING! WHAT IS YOUR WISH?" Aladdin looked up, hopeful.

"I want my wife and palace back," Aladdin cried, realizing he had, again, accidentally rubbed the ring.

"Only the genie of the lamp can grant you that," said the slave of the ring.

"The genie's in the palace," Aladdin said. "So take me there."

Instantly he found himself outside his palace, which was now in a strange land.

"Aladdin!" cried the princess, who had been weeping at her window.

Aladdin and the Magic Lamp

Aladdin raced to embrace her. She told him that she had given away the lamp—and immediately Aladdin knew the magician was behind it.

"I must have that lamp," Aladdin said.

"But the magician never lets it out of his sight," replied the princess, who in her captivity had learned the habits of the wicked man.

She and Aladdin came up with a plan.

That night, the princess asked the magician to dine with her. He gladly accepted and took a sip of the wine she offered him, which Aladdin had mixed with a poisonous powder. Instantly, the magician fell to the floor, dead.

Aladdin grabbed the lamp and, in no time at all, he, the princess, and the palace were back in China where they belonged. After the sultan died, they came to rule the kingdom and lived happily ever after.

Balloon Fun

Children love balloons! The first activity is educational, and a great introduction to experimenting and science. The suggestions that follow are a reminder of all the fun and simple things you can do with balloons. *(Remember that balloons present a choking hazard and supervise young children accordingly.)*

GAS BALLOON

balloon, empty bottle with a small neck, funnel, vinegar, baking soda

1. Placing the funnel into the mouth of the bottle, help your child put two teaspoons of baking soda into the bottle.
2. Pour $1/3$ cup of vinegar into the balloon using the funnel.
3. Stretch the neck of the balloon over the mouth of the bottle, pulling it on securely. You may want to hold onto the neck for support, since the reaction can sometimes be quite strong.
4. Hold the balloon upright to allow the vinegar to start mixing with the baking soda. The mixture should begin fizzing, expanding the balloon at an enormous rate.
5. You can explain to your child that gas is "hidden" in the baking soda. The gas that inflates the balloon is caused by the reaction between the vinegar, which is high in acetic acid, and the baking soda (also called sodium bicarbonate).

MORE BALLOON FUN

1. Blow a balloon up really big and then let it go. (Make sure you have enough room.)
2. Make wonderful noises by blowing up a balloon and releasing the air slowly while stretching the end of the balloon neck.
3. Rub an inflated balloon against a wooly sweater and then stick it to your hair.
4. Fill a small balloon with water for the bath or outdoors. Younger children love the feel of them in their hands.
5. Impress someone with this "magic" trick. Tape a small piece of scotch tape to an inflated balloon. If you stick a pin through the taped area, the balloon will not pop.

293

Knock knock!

Will you remember
me tomorrow?
Will you remember
me the next day?
Will you remember
me the next next day?

Knock Knock
> *Who's there?*

Hey! You've forgotten
me already!

Knock Knock
> *Who's there?*

Olive.
> *Olive who?*

Olive you, sweetie!

Knock Knock
> *Who's there?*

Lettuce.
> *Lettuce who?*

Lettuce in! Gotta use
the bathroom!

Knock Knock
> *Who's there?*

Cockadoodle.
> *Cockadoodle who?*

Cockadoodle WHO? No,
it's cockadoodle DOO!

Knock Knock
> *Who's there?*

Harry.
> *Harry who?*

Harry up and
open the door!

Knock Knock
> *Who's there?*

Betty.
> *Betty who?*

Betty-bye! Time
to go to bed!

Knock Knock
> *Who's there?*

Heaven.
> *Heaven who?*

Heaven you heard
enough knock knock
jokes yet?

Who's there?

Nourishing Soups

I am in love with soups. I always have this idea that they can become whole meals. These are simply the coziest. I found these soups at a farmer's market in Walnut Creek, a small town outside San Francisco. Hristo Kolev and his son, Raddy, were selling them. I have rarely tasted anything so fine. When Hristo sent me the recipes, I realized there are many variations and I have included them whenever I could. With a great crusty bread or Corn Bread *(page 162)* and a salad, you'll be the best dad cook in all the world.

Chicken Soup

2 cups diced celery
2 cups diced carrots
2 cups diced onions
3 cups diced leeks
1/4 lb butter
1 teaspoon of ground dried rosemary
1/2 teaspoon each dried basil, dried
    oregano, and dried thyme
3 bay leaves
1 cup of white wine (optional—remember
    alcohol dissipates in cooking)
4 chicken breasts, diced
3 quarts (14 cups) chicken broth
3 cups heavy cream
    salt and pepper to taste

1. In a large pot, saute the vegetables in the butter over medium heat until they are soft.
2. Add dried herbs and white wine and cook another 5 to 10 minutes.
3. Add chicken and broth, bring to boil, turn heat down, and simmer another 20 minutes.
4. Add cream, bring to a boil and turn off heat.
5. If the soup is too thin, add a "roux": Mix together 1/2 cup all-purpose flour with 1/2 cup soft butter. Roll into little balls and add as many balls as needed. This prevents those annoying little flour balls. (You can

use this trick to thicken gravy, too!)

6. Add salt and pepper to taste.

Serves 8 to 10
Can freeze for 4 weeks

As a variation, you can eliminate the cream and add a little chopped fresh italian parsley and grated Parmesan cheese before serving. Or you can add diced potatoes, rice, or pasta when you add the chicken to create a heartier meal.

Creamy Potato and Leek Soup

1 cup diced celery
2 cups diced onions
3 cups sliced leeks
1/2 cup butter
salt and pepper to taste
12 red potatoes or 6 large russet potatoes, quartered
2 1/2 quarts (12 cups) chicken broth
2 cups heavy cream
1/4 cup sour cream

1. In a large pot, saute the celery, onion, and leeks in the butter over medium heat until they are soft.
2. Add a pinch of salt and fresh ground pepper and cook for 3 to 4 minutes.
3. Add the potatoes and chicken broth and bring to a boil. Turn heat down and simmer until potatoes are soft. Turn off heat and let cool.
4. Process in the food processor until smooth.
5. Put the soup back on the stove and add the heavy cream and sour cream. Bring to a boil and then turn off heat.
6. Add salt and pepper to taste.

Serves 8 to 10
Can freeze for 4 weeks

Snowy Day Fun

As early winter's tiny snowflakes begin to drift past your window, tell your children that it's good luck to catch snowflakes on their tongues—it's the season's first snow activity, and it just might keep them entertained for a while. But as the snow begins to accumulate, there is more fun to be had, and outdoor playtime is a requisite. Don't forget snowball fights!

SNOW FAMILY
at least 4 inches of fresh snow, sticks, buttons

1. Start by making a snowball, and then rolling it around in the snow, changing directions every so often to make it nice and round. Keep rolling the ball in fresh snow until it's as large as you want it.
2. Make three snowballs: a large base, a medium body, a small head. Pile them on top of one another.
3. Use sticks for arms and buttons for eyes, nose, and mouth. Instead of making just one snowman, make an entire snow family modeled after your own. Dress up each snowperson with a personal belonging of each family member!

SNOW ANGELS
snow

1. Have your little angel lay on a fresh patch of snow.
3. He or she should go through the motion of "jumping jacks," but while laying on the ground.
3. Help your child get up carefully so as not to disturb the angel impression.

COLORED SNOW
snow, food coloring, spray bottle

1. Mix some food coloring in water, and then pour it into spray bottles.
2. Spray the colorful mixture onto the snow, drawing pictures or writing messages that will last . . . until the next snowfall.

Whether the weather be cold
or whether the weather be hot.
We'll weather the weather
whatever the weather
whether we like it or not.

or whether the

A Rainbow of Colors

Children love colors. Ask any young child his or her favorite color and he or she will give you a list of several colors. Painting would not be much fun if there was only black paint! Let your child thrill in the magic of colors with the following face and finger painting activities. Then explore the most wonderful colorful thing of all, a rainbow, by creating a few of your own.

MAKE A RAINBOW
deep baking pan, water, small mirror, flashlight, piece of white paper

1. Pour water in the baking pan.
2. Angle the mirror against the side of the pan so that a part of the mirror is not submerged in the water.
3. Shine the flashlight on the submerged part of the mirror.
4. While holding the light steady with one hand, hold the paper behind and above the light with the other. Your rainbow will be projected onto the paper. Trade places with your child and take turns making the rainbows.

FACE PAINTS
cornstarch, water, cold cream, food coloring, 6 small cups or a muffin tin, popsicle stick, paintbrush

1. Add 1 teaspoon cornstarch, $1/2$ teaspoon water, $1/3$ teaspoon cold cream, and a few drops of food coloring to each cup. Use a different color in each cup.
2. Stir with popsicle stick to mix color evenly. Hand your child the paintbrush, sit down, and let your child make a colorful Dad!

FINGER PAINTS
shaving cream, food coloring

1. Add different colors to mounds of shaving cream. That's it! The shaving

cream method is best to try out in the bathtub, where kids can make as much of a colorful mess painting on bathroom walls and each other as they want.

2. Turn on the water and clean up everything, including your children.

RAINBOW IN BOTTLES
6 clear, empty bottles; red, blue, and yellow food coloring

1. Fill the bottles with water. Add food coloring to each bottle, using each color for two bottles. Your child will love to watch as the dyes fall to the bottom, spreading out and coloring everything their wake. Explain to your child that red, blue, and yellow are primary colors.

2. When the colors have sufficiently settled, teach your child about secondary colors and color combinations. Add red to one blue bottle to make purple, yellow to a red bottle to make orange, blue to a yellow bottle to make green.

3. Let your child gently shake the bottles to finish coloring the water, and then sit the bottles in a place where the sun will shine through them.

FUN FACTS:
- A rainbow is created by sunlight passing through water droplets in the atmosphere after rain.
- Sunlight passing through water is broken up into the spectrum of colors to create the seven colors in a rainbow.
- The colors of the rainbow are always in the exact same order. The colors from the widest outside arch to the smallest inside arch closest to the horizon are red, orange, yellow, green, blue, indigo, and violet.

Rain

Rain, rain, go away,

Come again another day;

Little Johnny wants to play.

The Shoemaker and the Elves

nce upon a time there lived a very poor shoemaker. Though he made the best shoes in town, very few of his customers had enough money to pay him for them.

"Pay what you can afford," he would say, accepting such gifts as flowers or a chicken. "No one should have to go barefoot."

"You're a good man," his wife often said, as their customers walked away in shiny new shoes.

As time went on, the shoemaker became poorer and poorer until all he had left was enough leather for one pair of shoes. That evening he cut the leather and left it on his worktable. "I'll finish them in the morning," he said, turning out the light.

The next morning, the shoemaker and his wife woke to a great surprise! For there on the worktable was a finished pair of shoes. After closely examining the shoes, the shoemaker shook his head with wonder. "Every stitch is perfect!" he said. "Who could have done this?"

Just then, a richly dressed man entered the shop and tried the shoes on. "What a perfect fit!" he said, and paid the shoemaker

The Shoemaker and the Elves

enough money to buy leather for two more pairs of shoes.

That evening, the shoemaker cut the leather and planned to work on the shoes in the morning. But by morning, two finished pairs of shoes sat on the worktable.

This time, a richly dressed woman bought both pairs and gave the shoemaker so much money, he was able to buy enough leather for four pairs of shoes. Again, he cut the leather in the evening, and the shoes were finished by morning—this time, earning him enough money to buy leather for ten pairs of shoes!

After several weeks of this, the very poor shoemaker had become a very rich shoemaker. On the night before Christmas, after the leather had been cut, the shoemaker said to his wife, "Let's stay up tonight and see who's been making the shoes."

"Good idea!" said his wife. "We can light a lantern and hide behind the coatrack."

As the clock struck midnight, they watched in awe as ten tiny, naked elves marched into the shop and gathered round the worktable. Quickly and quietly, with deep concentration, they stitched and pierced and hammered until thirty perfect pairs of shoes sat lined up in a row. Then, quick as a wink, they marched out of the shop.

The Shoemaker and the Elves

"Those precious elves have made us rich!" said the shoemaker.

"They must be freezing!" said his wife. "I'm going to make ten tiny sets of clothes, using the best threads and patterns."

"And I'm going to make ten tiny pairs of shoes," said the shoemaker. "It's the least we can do to say thank you."

The next morning, the shoemaker and his wife got right to work. It didn't take long to make such tiny sizes, and they finished well before suppertime. That night, in place of leather, they laid out ten tiny shirts, ten tiny pairs of overalls, ten tiny snowsuits, ten tiny hats, ten tiny pairs of mittens, and ten tiny pairs of shoes. Then they lit the lantern and hid behind the coatrack.

At midnight, the shoemaker and his wife watched the ten tiny, naked elves march into the shop and gasp in delight! They loved the tiny outfits and giggled as they dressed. Then, in high, tinkling voices, they sang a thank-you song and danced a silly jig. At the first light of day, they skipped straight out the door—never to be seen again.

From that day on, the shoemaker's business did better than ever—though he still accepted yo-yo's, pinecones, and handkerchiefs when a customer couldn't afford to pay. Because, he and his wife agreed, no one should have to go barefoot.

Bye, baby bunting,

Father's gone a-hunting,

Mother's gone a-milking,

Sister's gone a-silking,

And brother's gone to buy a skin

To wrap the baby bunting in.

Bye, Baby Bunting

Chocolate Chip Cookies

Have you ever noticed how everyone is always trying to outdo everyone else when it comes to chocolate chip cookies? Try these! Another find from Hristo and Raddy— the father and son team from California. These are great served warmed and crumbled over vanilla ice cream.

2 sticks (1 cup) butter, softened
1 1/2 cups firmly packed brown sugar
1 cup white sugar
2 eggs
1 teaspoon vanilla extract
3 cups all purpose flour
1 teaspoon baking soda
1 teaspoon baking powder
15 oz (2 1/2 cups) chocolate chips

1. Preheat oven to 325°F.
2. Mix together butter and sugars until creamy. Add eggs and vanilla. Beat well.
3. In a separate bowl, combine flour, baking soda, and baking powder and gradually add to the butter mixture, mixing well.
4. Add chocolate chips and mix well.
5. Drop rounded tablespoonfuls unto ungreased or parchment-paper-covered cookie sheet, about 2 inches apart.
6. Bake 12 minutes until lightly browned. Do not over bake.
7. Transfer cookies to wire racks and let cool.

Makes about 3 dozen cookies

To make extra chocolatey chocolate chip cookies, add 1/2 cup cocoa powder and subtract 1/2 cup of the all-purpose flour. You can also add some white chocolate chips.

Chocolate Pudding

This creamy treat is better than instant and ridiculously easy to make. My father, George, didn't cook but, having been brought up in a highly cultured Hungarian family, he adored sweets and had great culinary taste. When I was eight years old he found a little Hungarian restaurant a few blocks from our home and we went there together for the chocolate pudding, just the two of us.

3/4 cup chocolate chips
1/2 cup sugar
2 cups whole milk
3 tablespoons cornstarch
pinch salt
1/2 tablespoon vanilla extract
1 cup heavy cream
1 teaspoon vanilla sugar (or sugar)

1. In a heavy saucepan, add chocolate, sugar and milk. Heat slowly over medium heat, whisking constantly until the chocolate is melted and smooth. Be careful not to let the mixture boil.
2. Turn off heat and pour half of the heated mixture into a bowl. Add cornstarch and salt and whisk until combined. Pour back into saucepan.
3. Keep stirring as you continue cooking over a low heat until mixture thickens, about 8 to 10 minutes.
4. Remove from heat, add vanilla extract, and let cool. You can accelerate the cooling by putting the saucepan in the refrigerator.
5. In a bowl, mix heavy cream and vanilla sugar. Whip with whisk or electric mixer until stiff.
6. Once the pudding has cooled, serve in a large bowl or in smaller individual bowls, and top with whipped cream.

Serves 4

Meringues

I know this doesn't sound like a guy thing but it is so good and so fast, and you can make so many different desserts out of it, I just couldn't help adding it. You will need a whisk or an electric mixer but it won't take more than ten minutes (plus the couple of hours in a slow oven).

4 egg whites (1/2 cup)
1/2 teaspoon cream of tartar
3/4 cup white sugar
3/4 cup powdered sugar

1. Preheat the oven to 200˚F.
2. In a mixing bowl, beat the egg whites until frothy. Add cream of tartar and beat at medium speed while slowly adding the sugar. Then beat at high speed until stiff peaks form when beater is raised slowly.
3. Spoon meringues onto parchment paper laid on a baking sheet or directly onto a Teflon baking sheet or glass baking dish. Do not butter or flour surface. You can make different shapes with meringues: divide meringue in half and make two cake-sized circles (after baking, put sliced strawberries and whipped cream on top of one circle and top with the other circle—then top with more strawberries and whipped cream); or shape the meringue into little bowls (after baking, fill with ice cream and chocolate sauce); or make cookie-sized meringues to be crumbled up and mixed with whipped cream and chocolate sauce.
5. Bake 2 to 2 1/2 hours. Do not let the meringues brown. If your oven has a pilot light, a better method is to make them the night before. Bake 1 hour at 200˚F, turn off the oven and leave in the oven until morning. They will be perfect.

Makes 1 cake,
6 bowls, or
20 meringues

Hansel and Gretel

Once upon a time there were a brother and sister named Hansel and Gretel who lived with their father, a woodcutter, and their evil stepmother. Their log house stood nestled on a daisy covered hillside overlooking a big forest.

Hansel was one year older than his sister, and made sure to look out for Gretel whenever they were together. He even shared his portion of bread with her at mealtime, though he was weak from hunger. You see, times had been hard in their part of the land, and the woodcutter had very few customers who could afford to buy his lumber. Over time, he had sold off nearly all their valuables to raise enough money to feed his family. Finally, the day came when he had nothing left to sell.

At the dinner table one evening, Hansel and Gretel's stepmother served four cold bowls of stew and bitterly announced, "This is the very last of our food. The pantry and cupboards are bare, and there is no money to buy any more. So make this bowl last, for I have no idea when the next bowl will come." With that, she sat down and loudly slurped down her portion of stew, which Hansel

Hansel and Gretel

could not help but notice was twice as large as everyone else's. As Gretel licked her bowl for any meager remains, her stomach let out a long growl that was loud enough for everyone to hear.

"What kind of a man lets his poor children starve?" cried out their father, "I am nothing but a failure who does not deserve the love of his family." Covering his face with his hands, he let out a great sob.

That night, as the woodcutter lay tossing and turning in bed, his wife whispered to him coldly, "We will all four die if something is not done quickly. There are just too many mouths to feed. Tomorrow we will take the children with us into the forest to chop wood. When it begins to get dark, we will leave them there alone and sneak home. They are far too young to find their way back out, and will surely die."

"Kill my own children!" boomed the woodcutter, "just to save myself?! Never!"

So his wife said nothing more about her plan and brought her husband a cup of tea to help him rest. The woodcutter drank it down gladly and fell into a deep, deep sleep. You see, his wife had mixed the tea with a special herb that causes anyone who swallows it to sleep for nearly a whole night and day.

Through the thin wall separating their own bedroom from their parents', Hansel and Gretel overheard their stepmother's beastly idea to abandon them. Frightened and confused, Gretel wept at the thought of starving to death in the woods. With tear-stained cheeks she wailed to her brother, "Oh Hansel, what shall become of us?"

"Have no fear, Gretel," Hansel assured her, "I won't let anything bad happen to you." And he gently squeezed her hand.

In the middle of the night, while his parents lay sleeping, Hansel snuck outside and collected handfuls of bright shiny stones that glittered in the moonlight like sparkling gems. He stuffed his pockets full of them before slipping silently back into bed.

The next morning, Hansel and Gretel's stepmother explained that their father was ill, and could not come out to collect wood. So the three of them set out into the forest without him, and worked late into the afternoon. When the sun dipped below the horizon, their stepmother built a fire for the children and told them to rest while she went to gather some twigs. But she never returned.

"Oh Hansel, we shall never find our way home!" cried Gretel.

"Have no fear, sister. I dropped a shiny pebble every few steps on our way here," said Hansel. "As soon as the moon rises it will reflect off the stones, making them twinkle like little stars. All we

have to do is follow them, and we'll be home before dawn."

Sure enough, when the moon appeared in the sky, Hansel and Gretel followed the pebbles home. As they arrived at the door of their little house, their father rushed outside and scooped them up in his arms. "My dear children!" he cried, "I thought you were lost forever! Thank goodness you're home safe."

Then their stepmother angrily scolded, "You naughty children! You ran off and I couldn't find you! I thought you'd been eaten by wild animals!"

A week later, the cupboards were bare again, and the children's stepmother made a plan to take the them even farther into woods, where they could never find their way home. That night, she drugged the woodcutter's tea again. But Hansel and Gretel knew what to do. Hansel tried to sneak out to collect more stones, but, alas, their stepmother had locked the front door!

"Oh Hansel, what shall we do?" cried Gretel.

"Have no fear, sister. I'll think of something," assured Hansel.

The next morning, the woodcutter's wife gave each of the children half a stale roll and took them deep into the forest. Again

Hansel and Gretel

she built them a fire as dusk set in, and again she left them, pretending to go in search of kindling. As the sky grew dark Gretel began to whimper in fear.

"Don't cry, Gretel," said Hansel, "I dropped crumbs from my bread every few steps on our way here. When the moon comes out it will reflect off the crumbs and we will follow them safely home."

But when the moon rose over the blackened sky, there were no crumbs left to be found. The birds in the forest had flown down and gobbled them all up!

"Surely we will die out here!" cried Gretel.

Even Hansel was a little worried, but he put up a brave front, telling Gretel, "Don't say such silly things. We will sleep here tonight by the fire, and find our way home tomorrow."

The next day, the children walked and walked, but could not find their way out of the thick, dark forest. As night descended, a light rain began to fall and a chilly wind whipped through the trees. The children had eaten nothing since sharing Gretel's bread the day before, and both were starving and tired. As supper time approached, Gretel dropped to ground, clutching her stomach in hunger. "Oh, Hansel," she cried, "I can go no farther. You must leave me here and go ahead."

Just then, a roll of thunder cracked loudly in the sky and a bolt of lightning lifted the forest's veil of darkness for a brief moment.

Hansel and Gretel

In that second, Hansel spied what looked like a little cottage not far ahead.

"Gretel, we are saved!" Hansel yelled, and he lifted her from the ground. As they neared the little house, the children saw that it was made not of wood and stone, but of gingerbread and candy! The roof was a layer of thick, white icing, and the windows were made of clear hardened sugar with shutters of chocolate. Gumballs and jellies trimmed the house, and a lovely white picket fence made of marshmallow surrounded the cottage.

The children's eyes went wide with glee. "Oh Hansel, we're in heaven!" exclaimed Gretel, as she ran to the fence and broke off a big piece. Hansel fell to his knees and dug out an m&m from the candy pathway leading to the front door.

Just then, a high piercing voice called out from the cottage, "Nibble, nibble like a mouse. Who's that nibbling at my house?"

Hansel replied, "It's just the wind blowing to and fro, back and forth, high and low."

No sooner had the children gone back to munching on the sweets, when a little old lady with white pasty skin and long black fingernails hobbled out of the cottage. Hansel and Gretel screamed in fright and began to run away but the old woman called out in the kindest voice, "Don't be afraid, my little friends. Come back and I'll fix you a hot delicious meal."

Hansel and Gretel

So Hansel and Gretel went inside the candy cottage and the old lady fed them hot apple pancakes with raisins and maple syrup. With their bellies full and warm, they snuggled into two small beds the old lady had made up, and she sang them a lullaby till they fell fast asleep.

While the children dreamt of gingerbread houses and white chocolate flowers, the old lady crept downstairs and pulled out a special cookbook from her bookshelf, titled *Child Delicacies*. She turned to a page with a recipe called "Little Boy Fricassee," and cackled with delight. You see, the old lady was really a wicked witch who only pretended to be kind to lure lost children into her home, where she could cook them up and eat them!

The next morning, the evil witch grabbed Hansel while he was still groggy with sleep and threw him into a large cage in her kitchen. Then she woke up Gretel with a hard shake. "Get up you lazy brat! Go cook your brother a tasty meal of fatty steak and milk. When he gets nice and plump, I'll bake him in my oven with carrots and potatoes. He'll be my most scrumptious child yet!" And she shoved the crying Gretel down the stairs.

For weeks, the wicked witch forced Gretel to feed her brother only the finest, richest foods. And every day she made Hansel stick out a finger for her to pinch, so she could see whether he was yet fat enough to eat. But the witch was nearly blind, and

Hansel and Gretel

Hansel cleverly stuck out a little chicken bone instead. Gradually, the old witch became more and more frustrated that Hansel was still so thin. After a month, she could wait no longer. "I don't care if you feel like skin and bones, you'll make a yummy morsel anyway!"

As the witch prepared a special basting sauce for Hansel, she instructed Gretel to put the bread in the oven to bake. Gretel was small, however, and her arms were too short to push the loaf in far enough. "You'll have to climb inside a little ways. Don't worry, I'll hold your legs, so you don't slip," coaxed the witch, with such a big smile her lips nearly cracked. But Gretel knew the old woman was trying to trick her so that she could shove her in the oven and cook her, too.

"I won't fit in the opening," insisted Gretel.

"You stupid girl," the witch snorted, "even I can get in there. See?" And the witch stuck her head and arms inside the broiling oven to demonstrate.

Quickly, Gretel gave the witch a big push, stuffing her whole body into the burning fire. The witch screamed as the flames surrounded her, but Gretel quickly shut the oven door and held her ears until the witch was dead.

Gretel then set her brother free from the cage and the two children danced and sang with joy.

Hansel and Gretel

They filled up two suitcases with piles of jewels and gold coins they found hidden in a chest under the old witch's bed, and set off for home.

Two days later, Hansel and Gretel finally found their way back out of the forest. Their father cried tears of joy when he laid eyes on them, and held them so close to his chest they could barely breath. The woodcutter's wife had been struck dead by a falling tree not two days after she abandoned the children, and their father had spent endless hours desperately searching the woods for his children.

"My beautiful son and daughter are alive and well," he wept, as he kissed the tops of their heads, "I'll never let you out my sight again."

The two children gave their father the treasures they'd found, and he sold them for so much money he never had to work again.

So Hansel and Gretel lived happily ever after with their father on the daisy covered hillside they'd grown up on, in the little log house the woodcutter had built.

And, do you know? They never touched another sweet again!

Is there anything sweeter than this?

—Anonymous

Starry Skies

S taring up at the night sky on a warm
summer night is one of the enduring
pleasures of life. Philosophers, poets, and
scientists alike have marveled at the cosmos,
musing about its beauty and origin. Maybe you
can't unravel the mysteries of the universe for
your children, but you can tell them the stories
of the stars and the constellations, those silent
sentinels who keep us company through the
night, and have for centuries held deep meaning
for different peoples of the world. A telescope is
not necessary to find the following constellations
—all that's needed is a beautiful, clear night, and
curious, young eyes and ears.

Hercules was a son of Zeus, and a favorite among the gods. He was forced to perform twelve impossible acts as punishment for killing his wife and children while ill with a temporary fit of insanity. By completing these tasks, he proved himself to be a *hero* —perhaps the greatest of Greek heroes—a word that is derived from his name.

Leo was a great lion whom Hercules was sent to kill in his first "impossible act." No weapon was able to pierce the lion's skin, and so Hercules, in order to kill him, trapped him inside a cave, and thrust his fist deep into Leo's throat. Once Hercules had taken the dead lion to show the king that he had succeeded, he used the hide as a protective shield to aid him in the rest of his twelve tasks.

Starry Skies

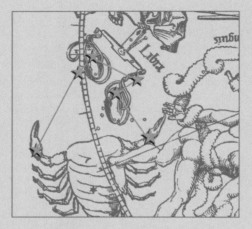

Libra is one of the signs of the zodiac, and has come to represent balance and justice. The constellation forms the "Scales of Justice" of Julius Caesar. Libra, as a constellation, is also part of Scorpius, and forms the claws of this great scorpion.

Pegasus was a winged horse that Zeus used to carry his thunderbolts and later placed among the stars. He was both a magical and playful creature, and his image today is recognized as a symbol of poetry.

Starry Skies

Sagittarius sits right in the heart of the Milky Way. Half man, half horse, this archer—according to mythology—was set in the skies to help navigators at sea find their way. He is also one of the signs of the zodiac.

Ursa Major and **Ursa Minor** are more commonly referred to as the Big Dipper and the Little Dipper, though if you look beyond this common arrangement of stars, you see that they are, in fact, both *bears*. Originally the mistress and son of Zeus (Callisto and Arcas), he changed them into animals to protect them from Hera, his wife, who was trying to kill them, and carried them into the sky by their long tails (these bears have longer tails than present-day bears, and these tails make up the handles of the big and little dippers). Hera convinced Poseidon (the sea god) not to let them bathe in the sea, and so they can be seen hovering just above the horizon, making them always visible in the night sky.

Twinkle Twinkle Little Star

by Jane Taylor

Twinkle, twinkle, little star,
How I wonder what you are!
Up above the world so high,
Like a diamond in the sky.

When the blazing sun is gone,
When he nothing shines upon,
Then you show your little light,
Twinkle, twinkle all the night.

Then the traveller in the dark,
Thanks you for your tiny spark,
He could not see which way to go
If you did not twinkle so.

In the dark blue sky you keep,
And often through my curtains peep,
For you never shut your eye,
'Til the sun is in the sky.

As your bright and tiny spark
Lights the traveller in the dark—
Though I know not what you are,
Twinkle, twinkle, little star.

All the Pretty Little Horses

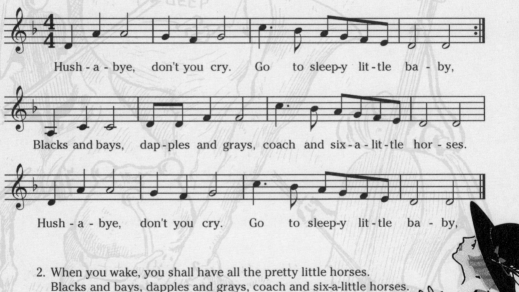

Hush - a - bye, don't you cry. Go to sleep-y lit-tle ba - by,

Blacks and bays, dap-ples and grays, coach and six-a-lit-tle hor - ses.

Hush - a - bye, don't you cry. Go to sleep-y lit-tle ba - by,

2. When you wake, you shall have all the pretty little horses.
   Blacks and bays, dapples and grays, coach and six-a-little horses.
   Hush-a-bye, don't you cry. Go to sleep-y little baby.

Hush Little Baby

Anonymous

Hush little baby, don't say a word,
Papa's going to buy you a mockingbird.

If that mockingbird won't sing,
Papa's going to buy you a diamond ring.

If that diamond ring turns brass,
Papa's going to buy you a looking glass.

If that looking glass gets broke,
Papa's going to buy you a billy goat.

If that billy goat won't pull,
Papa's going to buy you a cart and bull.

If that cart and bull fall down,
You'll still be the sweetest little baby in town.

JESSIE WILLCOX SMITH.

A Father's Numerology

Steven Lewis

Calculating Freedom

*Freedom's just another word
for nothing left to lose.*
—KRIS KRISTOFFERSON

In the weeks following Nancy's birth in 1973, I spent many late nights pacing the living room floor with our beautiful, fat, *howling* baby girl in my weary arms. On one of those long and harrowing sojourns nowhere, I found that I could control my frustration and maintain my sanity by calculating the years that it would take until the colicky baby would grow up—and I would be free again.

I figured that when Nancy reached eighteen—and Cael twenty-two—I would be free. Free, that is, to be me.

Me, the well-regarded writer and teacher I knew was my destiny. The day Nancy would leave for college to seek her destiny, I'd set sail on my own journey of self-actualization. I would be forty-five, still young enough to take advantage of the freedoms that would be mine simply by relinquishing my role as worrier and protector—and late-night pacer—a role she would no longer want me to serve. Nancy and I would be friends together in the real world of 1991, not Dada changing a messy diaper, or Daddy booting a soccer ball to his daughter, or even Dad pacing the living room at night waiting for the headlights in the driveway. We would be friends, talking politics or literature or whatever over a beer at Tony's Tavern.

A Fathers Numerology

That simple arithmetic helped me get through the colic that evening; and from that vantage point I could foresee a full life ahead to take care of my needs again—to go out when I wanted, to go to exotic places, to sleep late, to sleep long, to be me. Fathering two children, like going to college, was something I did en route to something else. My *real* identity was deeper, more complex than that. It just took some calculations.

And eighteen years later, when I woke up the morning after Nancy's first visit home from college, I remembered those simple calculations and understood with a tired yawn just how wrong they had been. What started out as a small hippie family of four, as you know, blossomed into a not-so-small tribe of seven kids who have defined life and freedom for me in ways I never envisioned on that night in 1973.

Yet all these years have shimmered past like a meteor and I still find myself awake in the middle of the night, up with Elizabeth, who has her own bad dreams, or growling at Bay and his friend Luke to "Go to sleep, now!" or listening almost breathlessly until I hear Danny walk through the front door after curfew.

Through my children's enduring presence, I know myself a little better now than I did when I paced the floor with Nancy all those years ago. I see more clearly my destiny today, even as I am

A Fathers Numerology

drawn ineffably toward the infinite. When people ask what I do, I still sometimes tell them out of habit or convenience—or some vestige of those days on North Newhall Street—that I am a writer and a teacher, wishing, I think, to add some unnecessary weight to my mere presence. But at the core of my pulsing heart I know I am not a writer or a teacher.

I am a father. I have been a father since I was a few steps out of my father's house. I have been a father for longer than it took John Keats to live a whole life and immortalize himself as a writer. I am a father when I stand in front of a class, when I sit at a computer screen, coach a Little League team, mow a lawn, plunge a toilet, read a poem, sing a song, sit on a beach . . . as I weep even as I laugh at it all. I will probably be lying awake, pacing the floor, arguing paradoxical points of childhood logic long after I am also a grandfather.

I am a father. That is all I am.

347

Sleep, Baby, Sleep

Sleep, ba - by, sleep, Your fa - ther's watch-ing his

sheep, Your moth - er shakes ___ the

dream - land tree, A lit - tle dream ___ falls

down for thee, Sleep, ba - by, sleep.

2. Sleep, baby, sleep,
The skies are full of sheep,
The little stars are the lambs, I guess,
The bright moon is the shepherdess,
Sleep, baby, sleep.

Make the most
of every day
For time does
not stand still.
One day this hand
will wave good-bye
While crossing
life's brave hill.

—Anonymous

Acknowledgments

"My Daughters," by Rick Bass, from *Fathering Daughters: Reflections by Men*, © 1998.

"Fatherhood" by Bill Cosby, copyright © 1986 by William H. Cosby, Jr. Used by permission of Doubleday, a division of Random House, Inc.

"Being a Father", copyright © 2000 by Winston Groom; by permission of his agents, Raines & Raines.

"Our Son," from *The Collected Verse of Edgar Guest* by Edgar Guest © 1984. Used with Permission of NTC/Contemporary Publishing Group, Inc.

"My Brother Bert," from *Meet My Folks* by Ted Hughes, Faber and Faber Ltd., publishers.

"The Mistake Game," © by Rodger Kamenetz. Used by permission of the author.

"A Father's Numerology: Calculating Freedom," from *Zen and the Art of Fatherhood* by Steven Lewis, copyright © 1996 by Steven Lewis. Used by permission of Dutton, a division of Penguin Putnam Inc.

"The Pony Man" by Gordon Lightfoot. © 1997 Moose Music Inc. (renewed). Used by permission.

"For the Love of My Children," © Kenny Loggins. Originally published in *Father and Son: the Bond* by Bill Hanson.

"The Hokey Pokey" words and music by Charles P. Macak, Taff Baker and Larry LaPrise. Copyright © 1950 (Renewed 1978) by Acuff-Rose Music, Inc. All rights reserved. Used by permission.

"Daddy Fell into the Pond" by Alfred Noyles. By permission of J.B. Lippincott and HarperCollins Publishers.

"Song to be Sung by the Father of Infant Female Children" by Ogden Nash. Copyright © 1933 by Ogden Nash, renewed. Reprinted by permission of Curtis Brown, Ltd.

"The Same River Twice" reprinted with permission of Simon & Schuster from *The Same River Twice: a Memoir* by Chris Offutt. Copyright © 1993 by Chris Offutt.

"The Bed Book" by Sylvia Plath. Text copyright © 1976 by Ted Hughes. By permission of HarperCollins Publishers.

"Transformations" by Tadeusz Rosewicz, from *Postwar Polish Poetry* by Czeslaw Milosz, copyright © 1965 by Czeslaw Milosz. Used by permission of Doubleday, a division of Random House, Inc.

"Oh, the Places You'll Go!" By Dr. Seuss. TM & copyright © by Dr. Seuss Enterprises, L.P. 1990. Reprinted by permission of Random House Children's Books, a division of Random House, Inc.

"A Prayer for Connection," © Samuel Shem. From *Fathering Daughters: Reflections by Men*. Used by permission of Samuel Shem.

"Rockabye," "One Two," and "Zebra Question" by Shel Silverstein. Copyright © 1981 by EVIL EYE MUSIC, INC. Used by permission of HarperCollins Publishers.

"Puff The Magic Dragon" words and music by Peter Yarrow and Leonard Lipton. Copyright © 1963 Pepamar Music Corp. Copyright renewed 1991 and assigned to Silver Dawn Music (ASCAP) and Honalee Melodies (ASCAP). All Rights on behalf of Honalee Melodies administered worldwide by Cherry Lane Music Publishing Company, Inc. Worldwide rights for Silver Dawn Music Administered by WB Music Corp. International Copyright Secured. All Rights Reserved.

ILLUSTRATIONS
pg. 10 & 57: Torrey; pg. 14-15 & 90: Ellen H. Clapsaddle; pg. 20 & 21: C. Twelvetrees; pg. 22-23 & 117 Shel Silverstein; pg. 28, 288: Margaret Evans Price; pg. 32, 176: Maurice E. Day; pg. 40-41: E.Curtis; pg. 42, 43, 228, 254, 296-297 & 343: Jessie Willcox Smith; pg. 49: S.B. Pearse; pg. 55: Kay; pg. 56, 292: Frank Hart; pg. 59: Josephine Bruce; pg. 60-61, 170: Randolph Caldecott; pg. 63: Florence M. Pettee; pg. 68, 160: M.E. Edwards; pg. 81: The P. & M. Co., Inc.; pg. 92, 310-311: Lunt Roberts; pg. 99: Edwin Morrow; pg. 110, 128: C.M. Burd; pg. 125: C.O.; pg. 145: H. Hoecker; pg. 159: Hansi; pg. 169: Allen Carter; pg. 179, 318: Hilda Cowham; pg. 187: M.Ames; pg. 202: Henry J. Johnson; pg. 212-213: Anne Rochester; pg. 236: Laurie Taylor; pg. 247: H.B.G; pg. 257: Kate Greenaway; pg. 266-267, 308-309: Hilda Austin; pg. 271: R.H. Porteous; pg. 305: Nelly Littlehale Umbstaetter; pg. 332-333: Fern Bisel Peat; pg. 339: Vernon Thomas; pg. 340-341: Joyce Mercer; pg. 348: Stephen W. Meader.